# "THE RESILIENT PROFESSIONAL:

## BALANCING PERFORMANCE, WELL- BEING, AND GROWTH"

**ISBN:** 978-93-6426-751-9
**Price:** ₹265.00
Publishing Year 2025

Published by:
**Crown Publishing**
Head Office: 3rd Floor, B.incube, Bilaspur,
Chhattisgarh 495006
Phones: +91 77228 14335
Email: publish@crownpublishing.in
Website: www.crownpublishing.in

# "THE RESILIENT PROFESSIONAL:

## BALANCING PERFORMANCE, WELL- BEING, AND GROWTH"

**By**

**AKSHAY KUMAR**

CROWN
PUBLISHING

## DISCLAIMER

The information contained in this publication is provided for general educational and informational purposes only. It is not intended as, and shall not be understood or construed as, medical, psychological, legal, financial, or any other form of professional advice. Readers should consult with a qualified healthcare provider, mental health professional, or other licensed specialist regarding any questions or concerns about their individual health, well-being, or workplace circumstances.

Neither the author nor the publisher makes any representations or warranties of any kind, express or implied, regarding the completeness, accuracy, reliability, suitability, or availability of the information contained herein. To the maximum extent permitted by applicable law, the author and publisher disclaim any liability for any direct, indirect, incidental, consequential, or special damages, losses, or injuries arising out of or in connection with the use of this publication, its content, or the application of the strategies discussed.

*This book is dedicated with deep respect to my parents, with love to my wife and my cute little boy. Everything I have in my life is because of their love and blessings.*

# *Table of Content*



*****

# INTRODUCTION

In today's fast-paced world, the demand of more and more output from an employee is sky high and so are the challenges that come with it. Balancing personal and professional life is one of the greatest among it. The concept of work-life balance which was once viewed as a luxury now has become an essential factor in ensuring overall well-being of an individual, particularly when it comes to mental health. This book seeks to explore the importance of mental health in the workplace, provide strategies for managing stress and offer actionable advice on how to achieve and maintain a healthy work-life balance.

As we delve into the pages of this book, we will uncover the complexities of modern work environment, how it impacts our mental and emotional well-being and also the practical steps which we can take to create a harmonious relationship between our work and life. The journey towards achieving work-life balance is not a "one-size-fits-all" process but with the right understanding, tools and mindset it is attainable for everyone.

## WHY MENTAL HEALTH AND WORK-LIFE BALANCE MATTERS

Mental health is a fundamental aspect of overall well-being yet it is often overlooked by most of us, especially in the context of our professional life. In the past, there was a clear boundary between work and personal life but this line has blurred over time, leaving many of us feeling overwhelmed, exhausted, and mentally drained.

Today, mental health is more than just the absence of illness; it encompasses emotional, psychological, and social well-being. It affects how we think, feel, and act both in our personal and professional lives. A strong mental state allows an individual to handle stress, relate to others and make decisions with clarity and confidence. However, when mental health is neglected it can lead to issues ranging from stress and anxiety to burnout and depression. All of these can severely impact one's ability to perform effectively at work and engage meaningfully in personal relationships.

Work-life balance on the other hand refers to one's ability to manage and fulfill both personal and professional responsibilities without compromising his physical and mental health or emotional well-being. It is the equilibrium where the demands of work do not encroach upon his personal time, relationships or self-care. It is important to achieve this balance if an individual wants to maintain his mental health because constantly doing overwork or having stress can lead to physical and emotional fatigue.

As work at the office grows, mental health, and work-life balance are increasingly intertwined. It has been observed that employees who maintain a healthy work-life balance tend to be more productive, engaged, and motivated. They are also less likely to experience mental health issues. On the contrary, when work-life balance is neglected the strain on mental health can become overwhelming and it leads to a cascade of problems that affect both professional performance and personal satisfaction.

Recent studies show that more than 70% of the employees experience some form of work-related stress and also their stress levels negatively impact their mental health. Long working hours, demanding deadlines and the pressure to be available all the time, create an environment that is conducive to mental health challenges. That is why it is essential for us to prioritize mental well-being and work-life balance; not just for personal satisfaction but for long-term professional success.

## THE MODERN WORKPLACE: NEW CHALLENGES FOR MENTAL HEALTH

The traditional workplace model has undergone through a significant change over the past few decades. The advent of new technologies, globalization, and shifting of corporate cultures has redefined work for us. Yes, these changes have brought few benefits (which we will also discuss later in the book) but they have also introduced new challenges, particularly regarding mental health. In today's connected world, the boundary between work and personal life has become increasingly blurred. With the rise of remote work and digital communication tools, employees are expected to be available around the clock, often leading to a 24/7 work culture. This has created a sense of constant pressure and obligation, where many of us struggle to "switch off" from work even during their personal time.

Moreover, the competition in the modern workplace is fiercer than ever. Many individuals feel the need to overextend themselves so that they can meet high expectations or secure their job in an uncertain economy. Job insecurity, long hours, tight deadlines, and ever-growing workloads has led to increased levels of stress and anxiety. Toxic work environments where employees face unreasonable demands or they don't get adequate support from management; only exacerbate these mental health issues.

Additionally, the popularity of remote work has also increased in this post - COVID time and it has brought with it a unique set of difficulties despite the flexibility it provides. Working from home, on one hand, eliminate commute stress and provide more personal time to an individual but on the other hand, it also lead to isolation and difficulty to manage time effectively. Most of the bosses think if an employee is working from home, he is in the peaceful and luxurious environment, where he can sleep, eat, do a little work and repeat. But in actual, they with their this mindset, put more pressure on the employees and make them work more than normal working hours compared to what they used to spent when they were operating from office. This has affected their work-life balance leading to the absence of social interaction, coupled with the pressures of balancing household responsibilities. Because of no or very less communication with colleagues and relatives they generate this feeling of loneliness, disconnection, and even reach to the stage of burnout.

And this is not only pertains to people working from home, those jobs which require working from traditional office setup, there also the pressure to maintain constant productivity, bringing more profits can result in chronic stress, which affects both mental and physical health of the employees. According to a research, chronic stress has been linked to various mental health disorders such as depression, anxiety, and panic attacks. It can also impair cognitive function, making it harder to concentrate, make decisions or solve problems effectively.

It is crystal clear that in modern workplace mental health is no longer a personal issue; it is a collective one that affects organizational success, team dynamics, and overall workplace culture. A healthy and happy employee can bring more productivity than ten unhappy and stressed employees. Then, think of what percentage of growth a company can achieve if all the company employees are stress-free and have good mental health. If their professional and personal life is balanced, they will be more enthusiastic towards their work and feel more dedicated towards their company. If a company do not prioritize employee mental health may face higher turnover rates - more and more employees will leave the company, as soon as they get an opportunity, even if the other job offers lesser pay. The productivity will decline on YOY basis, and if no one from top management considers mental health of employees as a key factor, their profits will keep decreasing. On the flip side, if an organization invests in mental health initiatives and foster a supportive environment often it will see improved performances, innovations, job satisfaction among employees and ultimately the productivity will shoot upwards.

## HOW TO USE THIS BOOK

This book is designed for understanding the complex relationship between mental health and work-related stress and also how to achieve work-life balance. It provides practical advices, strategies, and real-life examples to help readers navigate the challenges of modern work while prioritizing their mental well-being.

Each chapter of this book addresses a different aspect of work-related mental health and balance, starting with an understanding of the challenges we face in the modern workplace and moving towards practical solutions for building resilience, managing stress, and prioritizing mental health. Whether you are an entry-level employee or a seasoned professional, this book provides guidance tailored to different career stages and personal needs.

Ultimately, the goal of this book is not just to help you manage stress in the workplace but to empower you to take control of your mental health and find a sustainable way to thrive in both your professional and personal life.

# CHAPTER 1

# THE MODERN WORKPLACE AND ITS IMPACT ON MENTAL HEALTH

The modern workplace has evolved rapidly in recent years. The technological advancement and societal shifts have led to fundamental changes in the way we work. While these changes have brought increased efficiency, flexibility, and opportunities in our professional life, they have also presented new challenges for the employees, particularly concerning about their mental health. This relentless pace of today's work culture, the rise of remote work and the increase in blurriness of boundaries between personal and professional life have placed an unprecedented pressure on workers. In this chapter, we will explore how the modern workplace has impacted our mental health, drawing on statistics, case studies, and expert insights to provide a comprehensive understanding of this complex issue.

## Section 1: The Pressure of the 24/7 Work Culture

### 1.1 The Impact of Technology on Work-Life Boundaries

Technology has revolutionized the workplace. It has made it easier for us to communicate, collaborate, and manage multiple tasks simultaneously. However, this constant connectivity has also diminished the lines between work and personal life. The so-called gifts of modernization i.e. smart phones, emails, instant messaging apps, and project management apps have allowed the employees to be reachable at any time regardless of their location. This "always-on" culture has created an environment where workers feel obligated to be available and responsive, even if they are outside of their traditional work hours.

In earlier days, the end of the workday used to mark a clear boundary between professional and personal time. Employees would leave the office on time and the workday was simply over. No employer used to call, message or mail his employees after they have left for their home. There was "wisdom" of respecting one's personal or family time and that's why people used to love their jobs, no matter how harsh or labor inducing it was. But today, the expectation of being available for 24/7 has significantly disrupted this dynamic. A study conducted by a psychological association found that nearly 60% of employees check their work related emails and messages after working hours; often during evenings, weekends or even while on vacation. This constant engagement with work tasks contributes to increased stress, anxiety, and difficulty disconnecting from the demands of the job.

## 1.2 The social expectation of constant productivity

Beyond technological advancement, social changes have also contributed to the pressure of modern work culture. The rise of hustle culture and the glorification of constant productivity have normalized the idea that success requires working long hours, often at the expense of personal well-being. The idea of late sitting has made so generalized that most of the employees now have adapted to it, for them 10-12 hours a day is normal working hours. Moreover, beyond that also they keep themselves available of mobile phones for their employer. Many employees feel that they need to over-perform, take on extra tasks and demonstrate dedication towards their employers by being accessible and responsive at all times. This may bring them good appraisal or promotions in short duration but this also results in them with no social or personal life - No friends, family or relationship.

Social media also plays a significant role in amplifying these pressures. They often showcase images of people working late into the night are celebrating professional accomplishments. This creates a distorted perception that everyone else is constantly working and achieving, leading individuals to feel inadequate if they aren't doing the same. This fear of falling behind, combined with the societal expectation to "grind," can fuel feelings of inadequacy, burnout, and overwhelm.

## 1.3 The Psychological Toll of the 24/7 Work Culture

The psychological toll of the 24/7 work culture is profound. Workers who feel pressured to be constantly productive are more likely to experience chronic stress, anxiety, and burnout. This sense of always being "on" can disrupt sleep, hinder the ability to relax and reduce overall life satisfaction.

Psychologically, the lack of separation between work and personal life creates what is known as "role conflict," where individuals struggle to balance competing demands from both spheres. Role conflict often leads to feelings of frustration, guilt, and dissatisfaction, as people feel they are failing to meet the expectations of their jobs, families, and personal goals simultaneously. This can also lead to a lack of time for self-care, further exacerbating mental health challenges.

Additionally, research has shown that employees who feel they must always be connected to work are more likely to experience symptoms of anxiety and depression. A study says that workers who reported higher levels of after-hours connectivity were more likely to experience emotional exhaustion, stress-related sleep disturbances, and overall lower levels of well-being.

For many employees, the solution to these challenges lies in creating clear boundaries around work and personal time. However, setting these boundaries can be difficult in a culture that often rewards overwork and penalizes those who are not always available. As a result, many employees continue to struggle with maintaining a healthy work-life balance, leading to long-term mental health consequences.

## Section 2: Workplace Stress and Mental Health

### 2.1 Mental Health Statistics in the Modern Workplace

Workplace stress and its impact on mental health are major concerns for both employees and the employers. The World Health Organization (WHO) estimated that depression and anxiety cost the global economy approximately $1 trillion in lost productivity each year. Additionally, mental health issues in the workplace are on the rise. According to a 2023 survey over 80% of employees reported some level of work-related stress. More terrifying thing was that most of them didn't even know that they are experiencing stress and this could lead to burnout or other mental health issues. Nearly 35% of respondents stated that their work stress had increased significantly over the past few years, with many citing factors such as heavy workloads, tight deadlines, and lack of support from management as the contributing factors.

## 2.2 Burnout: The Silent Epidemic

Burnout is a state of emotional, physical, and mental exhaustion caused by prolonged exposure to stress. It has become increasingly prevalent in the modern workplace. The World Health Organization has officially recognized burnout as an "occupational phenomenon," further highlighting the seriousness of this issue.

The symptoms of burnout include chronic fatigue, reduced productivity, irritability, and feelings of detachment or cynicism toward one's work. Employees who experience burnout are often unable to perform at their best and with time, their mental health deteriorates. Burnout can lead to anxiety disorders, depression, and even physical health issues such as high blood pressure and weakened immune systems.

As per a survey, 70% of employees reported feeling burnout at least some of the time, with nearly 30%

experiencing burnout "very often" or "always." This phenomenon is not limited to any specific industry or job role—it affects employees at all levels, from entry-level workers to top executives. Airline industry, which in my view is the epitome of hospitality business, recently, we have seen many of their workers engaging in heated arguments with their customers. Many of the conversations with customer care executives result in abuse or fight. And we can see many such examples in various fields in our day to day life. All of this is due to constant increasing work pressure and demands from the top management for more productivity and profits.

## 2.3 Anxiety and Depression in the Workplace

Anxiety and depression are two of the most common mental health issues experienced by employees in the modern workplace. The constant pressures of meeting deadlines, managing workloads, and navigating office politics can exacerbate feelings of anxiety. For some employees, workplace stress may trigger or worsen pre-existing mental health conditions.

A study in 2023 found that nearly one in five employees reported experiencing symptoms of clinical anxiety, with many attributing their symptoms to work-related stressors. Additionally, over 30% of employees reported feeling depressed, with work overload being a significant contributing factor to their mental health struggles.
Depression can manifest in the workplace in several ways, including decreased motivation, difficulty

concentrating, irritability, and withdrawal from colleagues. Employees who struggle with depression may find it challenging to meet performance expectations, leading to further stress and exacerbating their symptoms. In some cases, untreated depression can lead to absenteeism or presenteeism*, where employees are physically present at work but unable to perform effectively due to their mental health condition.

## Section 3: The Rise of Remote Work: Pros and Cons for Mental Health and Work-Life Balance

### 3.1 The Shift to Remote Work

Remote work has become a prominent feature of the modern workplace, especially after COVID-19 pandemic. Many companies have adopted remote work policies to accommodate employees' needs for flexibility and safety. For some, remote work has provided much-needed relief from long commutes, rigid office schedules and the distractions of a traditional office environment. However, while remote work offers numerous benefits, it also presents unique challenges for mental health and work-life balance.

### 3.2 The Benefits of Remote Work for Mental Health

Remote work offers few mental health benefits too, particularly in terms of increased flexibility and autonomy. Many employees report that working from home allows them to create a more personalized work environment - free from the distractions and pressures of an office setting. As per them, the online meetings are far less hectic than the physical meetings in the conference hall of the office. Though online meetings don't have any already planned schedule like offline ones and can start any time of the day, but still they are in the convenience of a cozy corner of the home as compared to the torture cell of the office. Remote workers often have more control over when to work and when to take breaks, enabling them to have better balance professional responsibilities with personal obligations. Due to this flexibility of remote work which allows employees to take break when needed, engage in self-care activities and spend more time with family or pursuing hobbies. This increased work-life integration can lead to reduced stress and improved mental well-being.

For individuals who struggle with social anxiety or sensory overload, remote work can offer a reprieve from the challenges of navigating a crowded office. Additionally, the elimination of commuting time can lead to improved mood and energy levels, as employees are able to spend more time on activities that bring them joy and fulfillment.

### 3.3 The Challenges of Remote Work for Mental Health

While remote work offers above mentioned advantages, it also presents challenges, particularly when it comes to maintaining boundaries between work and personal life. Without the clear physical separation of the office, many remote workers find it difficult to "switch off" from work mode. The temptation to check emails, respond to messages or finish up tasks outside of traditional work hours can lead to overwork and burnout.

Remote work can also lead to feeling of isolation and loneliness, as employees miss out on the social interactions and camaraderie that come with working in an office. For some, the lack of face-to-face contact with colleagues can result in a sense of disconnection and detachment from the organization. This isolation can exacerbate feelings of anxiety and depression, particularly for individuals who rely on social interactions for emotional support.

Moreover, remote workers may face challenges related to productivity and motivation. Without the structure of an office environment, some employees struggle to stay focused and manage their time effectively. This can lead to increased stress and frustration, as workers may feel they are not meeting their own or their employer's expectations.

To navigate these challenges, remote workers must establish clear boundaries around work hours, create a dedicated workspace and prioritize regular social interactions, whether through virtual meetings or in-person gatherings with friends and family.

- **Case Studies: Individuals Struggling with Modern Work Demands**

### 4.1 Sarah: A Marketing Professional Facing Burnout

Sarah, a 35-year-old marketing manager who had always been a high achiever. She loved her job and was known for her creativity, dedication, and ability to meet tight deadlines. However, as her company expanded, so did her responsibilities. Soon, Sarah found herself working late into the night, answering emails on weekends, and feeling overwhelmed by the constant pressure to deliver results.

Months after months of pushing herself to the brink, Sarah began to experience symptoms of burnout. She felt exhausted all the time, struggled to concentrate, and started to dread going to work each day. Despite her best efforts, her productivity declined and she found herself making mistakes she would never have made before. Now, she has started hating the job, she once loved. Daily she had to drag herself to work, work tirelessly and come home only to sleep.

Sarah's burnout eventually led to a breakdown, forcing her to take a medical leave of absence to focus on her mental health. But Sarah was lucky enough to have good employer, her boss suggested her a therapist and with the help of the therapist, Sarah learned how to set boundaries, prioritize self-care and manage her workload more effectively. She returned to work with a renewed sense of purpose and a commitment to maintaining a healthier work-life balance.

## 4.2 Vipul: A Software Engineer Grappling with Remote Work Isolation

Vipul, a 28-year-old software engineer, had always thrived in an office environment. He enjoyed collaborating with colleagues, brainstorming ideas and being part of a team. However, when his company shifted to remote work during the COVID-19 pandemic, Vipul found himself struggling with the isolation of working from home.

Without the daily interactions with his coworkers, Vipul felt increasingly lonely and disconnected. His motivation waned and he began to feel anxious about his performance. Despite his best efforts to stay engaged through virtual meetings, Vipul found it difficult to maintain the same level of productivity he had in the office.

Vipul's mental health began to deteriorate and he realized that he needed to take action to address his feelings of isolation. He started scheduling regular video calls with his colleagues, joined online communities for software engineers and made an effort to connect with friends outside of work. These changes helped Vipul regain a sense of connection and improve his mental well-being, allowing him to thrive in the remote work environment.

## Conclusion

The modern workplace presents a complex landscape of opportunities and challenges for mental health. While technology and remote work have introduced flexibility and autonomy, they have also blurred the boundaries between work and personal life, leading to increased stress, burnout and mental health issues. The pressure to be constantly available and being over productive has created an environment where employees are at risk of experiencing anxiety, depression and emotional exhaustion.

By recognizing the impact of the 24/7 work culture, understanding the mental health challenges associated with modern work demands, and learning from real-life examples, individuals and organizations can take steps to prioritize mental well-being.

# CHAPTER 2

# UNDERSTANDING MENTAL HEALTH AND WORK-RELATED STRESS

Work-related stress is one of the most pervasive and significant contributors to mental health challenges in today's dynamic work environments. While some level of stress is natural in any workplace, but long-term stress due to late sitting, meeting deadlines, and always multitasking can cause a number of mental health problems, including anxiety, depression, and burnout. As organizations continue to push for higher productivity and employees struggle to balance their professional and personal lives it is important to understand the various types of work-related stress, their impact on mental health, and how it affects cognitive function.

This chapter delves into the complexities of work-related stress, exploring its different forms, the mental health disorders it can aggravate, and how chronic stress can impair cognitive abilities such as memory, decision-making, and productivity. Additionally, we will identify key signs of overworking and strategies for recognizing when stress is negatively impacting your mental well-being.

## Section 1: Types of Work-Related Stress

Work-related stress comes in many forms, affecting employees differently depending on their work environment, roles, and personal situations. However, four main types of stress commonly emerge: performance anxiety, job insecurity, toxic workplace environments, and burnout. Each type of stress has its own triggers, symptoms, and long-term effects on mental health.

### 1.1 Performance Anxiety

Performance anxiety in the workplace stems from the pressure to meet deadlines, exceed expectations, and achieve specific targets. In highly competitive industries, employees often feel they are under constant scrutiny, with their performance evaluated on a daily or even hourly basis. This type of stress is especially prevalent in roles where success is measured by numbers–whether it's sales targets, customer satisfaction scores, or project deadlines.

Performance anxiety manifests in various ways, including fear of failure, perfectionism, and the constant worry of being judged or criticized by supervisors and colleagues. The Employees experiencing performance anxiety may have trouble sleeping, feel irritable or agitated, and struggle to concentrate on tasks.

The pressure to perform can also create a cycle of overworking, where employees put in long hours to compensate for their perceived shortcomings or to keep up with demanding expectations. Over time, this constant state of tension can lead to physical symptoms such as headaches, fatigue, and digestive issues, as well as mental health problems like anxiety and depression.

**Strategies to Manage Performance Anxiety:**

- **Set realistic goals:** Break down large projects into smaller and manageable tasks. Focus on progress rather than perfection.
- **Practice self-compassion:** Remind yourself that mistakes are a natural part of growth and learning.
- **Develop time-management skills:** Prioritize tasks and allocate specific time slots to work on them, which can reduce the overwhelming feeling of having too much on your plate.
- **Seek feedback constructively:** Instead of fearing criticism, approach feedback as an opportunity for improvement.

## 1.2 Job Insecurity

Job insecurity is another common form of work-related stress, particularly in industries which are undergoing rapid changes or downsizing. Economic instability, technological advancements, and corporate restructuring can make employees feel uncertain about the future of their jobs. The fear of layoffs, demotions, or pay cuts can lead to chronic stress, anxiety, and a lack of motivation.

There are two scenarios when employees feel insecure about their job prospects, one when they may begin to disengage from their work, experience reduced productivity, or develop a sense of helplessness. Second, when they may start working beyond their physical and mental limitations to cope up with other colleagues and save his job. Both scenarios can exacerbate feelings of low self-worth, as employees may internalize the possibility of job loss as a reflection of their value or competence.

Research has shown that prolonged job insecurity can lead to a variety of mental health problems, including depression, anxiety, and even substance abuse. The constant worry about the stability of one's career can also spill over into personal life, straining his relationships and also affecting overall life satisfaction.

**Strategies to Manage Job Insecurity:**

- **Focus on what you can control:** While job security may be out of your hands, improving your skills, networking, and staying informed about industry trends can increase your employability.
- **Build a financial safety net:** Having savings or a backup plan can reduce the stress of potential job loss.
- **Communicate with supervisors:** Ask for clarity regarding your job role and future opportunities. Open communication can sometimes alleviate uncertainties.
- **Seek support from colleagues:** Sharing your concerns with trusted colleagues or friends can provide emotional relief and practical advice.

## 1.3 Toxic Workplace Environments

A toxic workplace environment is characterized by poor communication, lack of support, unfair treatment, and unhealthy competition. In such environments, employees may experience bullying, harassment, or discriminatory behavior, leading to feelings of isolation and distress. Toxic workplaces foster a culture of blame, fear, and negativity, which can have profound effects on mental health.

In addition to emotional distress, employees in toxic environments may experience physical symptoms such as headaches, fatigue, and digestive problems. Long-term exposure to such environments can lead to chronic stress, anxiety, depression, and in severe cases, post-traumatic stress disorder (PTSD).

Toxic workplaces are particularly harmful because they often perpetuate a cycle of stress and disengagement. When employees feel unsupported or unappreciated, their productivity and job satisfaction decline, which can lead to further negative feedback or mistreatment from management.

**Strategies to Manage a Toxic Workplace:**

- **Document incidents:** Keep a record of any inappropriate behavior, harassment, or unfair treatment, which can be helpful if you need to report issues to HR or seek legal advice.
- **Set boundaries:** Protect your mental health by setting boundaries with difficult colleagues or supervisors. Limit your exposure to negative influences.
- **Seek support:** Reach out to trusted coworkers, friends, or a therapist to process your emotions and develop coping strategies.

- **Explore other opportunities:** If the toxicity is unbearable and unlikely to change, consider looking for a new job that aligns with your values and offers a healthier environment.

## 1.4 Burnout

Burnout is a state of physical, emotional, and mental exhaustion caused by prolonged exposure to stress. It is often the result of overworking, lack of rest, and an inability to disconnect from job responsibilities. Employees experiencing burnout may feel drained, detached from their work, and unable to meet performance expectations.

Burnout affects not only mental health but also physical health. Symptoms include chronic fatigue, headaches, digestive issues, insomnia, and weakened immunity. On a mental level, burnout can lead to feelings of hopelessness, cynicism, and irritability. Over time, it can contribute to anxiety disorders, depression, and even substance abuse.

Burnout is particularly prevalent in high-stress industries, such as healthcare, finance, and education, where employees often face unrealistic demands and long working hours. However, it can occur in any profession where there is a lack of balance between work and personal life.

### Strategies to Prevent Burnout:

- **Take regular breaks:** Schedule short breaks throughout the day to recharge and prevent mental exhaustion.

- **Practice mindfulness:** Mindfulness techniques, such as meditation or deep breathing, can help you stay grounded and reduce stress levels.
- **Set boundaries:** Learn to say no when your workload becomes unmanageable, and set clear boundaries around work hours.
- **Prioritize self-care:** Engage in activities that bring you joy and relaxation outside of work, such as exercise, hobbies, or spending time with loved ones.

## Section 2: Mental Health Disorders Affected by Work

Work-related stress can exacerbate or contribute to the development of several mental health disorders. While stress is a natural response to demanding situations, chronic stress can trigger or worsen conditions such as depression, anxiety, and panic disorders. Understanding how these mental health issues are affected by work stress is essential for recognizing when to seek help and taking steps to manage stress effectively.

### 2.1 Depression

Depression is one of the most common mental health disorders, affecting millions of people worldwide. Work-related stress, particularly from factors such as job insecurity, performance anxiety, and toxic workplace environments, can contribute to the onset or worsening of depression.

Symptoms of depression include persistent sadness, loss of interest in activities, difficulty concentrating, and feelings of hopelessness. In the workplace, depression can lead to absenteeism, presenteeism (being physically present but unable to perform effectively), and a decline in job performance.

Employees experiencing depression may also struggle with feelings of guilt or shame about their inability to meet work expectations. This can create a vicious cycle, where the stress of work exacerbates depression, and the symptoms of depression, in turn, worsen work performance.

**Strategies to Manage Depression at Work:**

- **Seek professional help:** Therapy or counselling can provide valuable support in managing depression.
- **Take time off if needed:** If depression becomes overwhelming, consider taking a leave of absence to focus on your mental health.
- **Communicate with your employer:** If possible, discuss your mental health with your supervisor or HR department to explore accommodations or adjustments to your workload.

## 2.2 Anxiety

Anxiety disorders are characterized by excessive worry, fear, and tension. In the workplace, anxiety can be triggered by factors such as tight deadlines, high workloads, and performance pressure. Employees with anxiety disorders may experience panic attacks, difficulty concentrating, and physical symptoms such as sweating, rapid heartbeat, and shortness of breath.

Work-related anxiety can be particularly challenging because it often feeds on the need for perfectionism and fear of failure. Employees with anxiety may constantly second-guess their work, worry about how they are perceived by colleagues, and struggle with imposter syndrome.

**Strategies to Manage Anxiety at Work:**

- **Practice grounding techniques:** Techniques such as deep breathing or progressive muscle relaxation can help reduce anxiety in stressful situations.
- **Break tasks into smaller steps:** Tackling projects one step at a time can make them feel more manageable and reduce feelings of overwhelm.
- **Use time management tools:** Organizational tools, such as to-do lists or project management apps, can help you stay on top of tasks and reduce anxiety about deadlines.

## 2.3 Panic Disorders

Panic disorders involve recurrent panic attacks, which are sudden episodes of intense fear or discomfort. These attacks can be triggered by workplace stressors such as performance evaluations, public speaking, or tight deadlines.

During a panic attack, employees may experience symptoms such as rapid heartbeat, shortness of breath, dizziness, and a feeling of impending doom. Panic attacks can be debilitating, making it difficult to focus on work tasks or engage with colleagues.

**Strategies to Manage Panic Disorders at Work:**

- **Develop a coping plan:** Work with a therapist to develop coping strategies for managing panic attacks in the workplace.
- **Create a calming environment:** If possible, personalize your workspace with calming elements, such as plants, soothing colors, or aromatherapy.
- **Take breaks:** If you feel a panic attack coming on, step away from your desk and practice relaxation techniques until you feel calmer.

## Section 3: How Stress Impacts Cognitive Function

Stress doesn't just affect emotional well-being; it also has a significant impact on cognitive function. When we experience stress, our bodies release stress hormones such as cortisol, which can interfere with brain processes related to memory, decision-making, and productivity.

### 3.1 Memory

Chronic stress can impair both short-term and long-term memory. High levels of cortisol can disrupt the brain's ability to form new memories and retrieve existing ones. Employees under constant stress may find it difficult to remember important details, complete tasks accurately, or retain information from meetings.

In some cases, stress-induced memory problems can lead to more serious cognitive issues, such as difficulty concentrating, brain fog, and mental fatigue.

This can result in decreased productivity, mistakes, and a decline in job performance.

**Strategies to Improve Memory under Stress:**

- **Practice stress-reduction techniques:** Mindfulness, meditation, and deep breathing can help reduce cortisol levels and improve memory.
- **Stay organized:** Use tools such as to-do lists, calendars, and reminders to keep track of important tasks and deadlines.
- **Get adequate sleep:** Sleep is essential for memory consolidation, so prioritize getting enough rest each night.

## 3.2 Decision-Making

Stress can also impair decision-making abilities. When we are stressed, our brains tend to focus on immediate threats or problems, making it difficult to think clearly or consider long-term consequences. Employees under stress may make hasty decisions, overlook important details, or struggle to evaluate different options effectively.

In high-pressure situations, stress can lead to a state of cognitive overload, where the brain becomes overwhelmed by too much information. This can result in poor judgment, impulsive actions, and increased errors.

**Strategies to Improve Decision-Making under Stress:**

- **Take breaks before making important decisions:** Stepping away from a problem for a few minutes can help clear your mind and allow for more thoughtful decision-making.

- **Seek input from others:** Consulting with colleagues or mentors can provide new perspectives and reduce the pressure to make decisions alone.
- **Use decision-making frameworks:** Tools such as pros and cons lists, flowcharts, or decision trees can help structure your thinking and make the process more manageable.

### 3.3 Productivity

While some people believe that stress can enhance productivity, chronic stress often has the opposite effect. Prolonged exposure to stress can lead to mental exhaustion, burnout, and a decline in overall work performance. Employees who are stressed may struggle to complete tasks efficiently, make more mistakes, and find it difficult to stay motivated.

Stress can also lead to procrastination, as employees may avoid tasks they find overwhelming or anxiety-inducing. This can create a cycle of increased stress, as deadlines pile up and responsibilities become harder to manage.

**Strategies to Improve Productivity under Stress:**

- **Break tasks into smaller steps:** Large projects can feel overwhelming, so break them down into manageable chunks and focus on one task at a time.

- **Prioritize tasks:** Use tools like the Eisenhower Matrix to prioritize tasks based on urgency and importance, allowing you to focus on high-impact work.
- **Schedule regular breaks:** Taking short breaks throughout the day can help prevent mental fatigue and keep you energized.

## Section 4: Signs You're Overworking

Overworking can have serious consequences for both physical and mental health. While it's natural to put in extra hours during busy periods, consistently overworking can lead to burnout, exhaustion, and a decline in overall well-being. Recognizing the signs that work is negatively impacting your mental health is the first step toward making changes to protect yourself from long-term harm.

### 4.1 Constant Fatigue

One of the most common signs of overworking is constant fatigue. If you find yourself feeling tired even after a full night's sleep, it may be a sign that you're pushing yourself too hard. Chronic fatigue can impair concentration, decision-making, and productivity, making it difficult to perform at your best.

### 4.2 Irritability and Mood Swings

Work-related stress can take a toll on emotional well-being, leading to irritability, mood swings, and difficulty managing emotions. If you find yourself becoming easily frustrated with colleagues, snapping at loved ones, or feeling on edge, it may be a sign that stress is overwhelming your ability to cope.

### 4.3 Difficulty Disconnecting from Work

If you find it hard to disconnect from work even during off-hours, it may be a sign that work is taking over your life. Employees who are overworked often feel compelled to check emails, work on projects, or think about work-related tasks during evenings, weekends, and vacations. This constant connection to work can prevent you from fully relaxing and recharging, leading to burnout.

### 4.4 Physical Symptoms

Work-related stress can manifest in physical symptoms such as headaches, digestive issues, muscle tension, and insomnia. If you notice a pattern of physical ailments that seem to worsen during periods of high stress, it's important to take action to manage your workload and prioritize self-care.

## Conclusion

Understanding the types of work-related stress, their impact on mental health, and the effects of stress on cognitive function is crucial for maintaining well-being in the modern workplace. By recognizing the signs of overworking and taking steps to manage stress, both employees and employers can create healthier, more sustainable work environments.

# CHAPTER 3

# FINDING YOUR BALANCE: PRIORITIZING MENTAL HEALTH

In today's demanding work environments, finding balance between professional responsibilities and personal well-being is crucial for long-term mental health. However, achieving this balance is not a one-size-fits-all process. It requires self-awareness, the ability to set boundaries, and a conscious effort to develop routines that prioritize both work and life outside of the office.

This chapter will explore how to find that balance by diving into key strategies such as setting boundaries, developing self-awareness, creating a balanced routine, and understanding the nuances of work-life balance across different career stages.

## Section 1: Setting Boundaries: Why Boundaries Are Essential and How to Set Them

Boundaries serve as the foundation for maintaining a healthy work-life balance. Without clear boundaries, the lines between work and personal life blur, leading to chronic stress, burnout, and emotional exhaustion. Many employees find themselves answering emails late at night, skipping meals, or sacrificing family time in order to meet work demands. While occasional extra effort may be required, consistently neglecting personal needs for the sake of work can have long-term negative effects on mental health.

## 1.1 Why Boundaries Are Essential

Boundaries are essential because they protect your mental health by creating clear divisions between your work life and your personal life. When you set boundaries, you communicate your limits to your employer, colleagues, and even yourself. This prevents overwork and ensures that you have time to recharge and focus on your well-being.

Boundaries also help reduce resentment and burnout. Without boundaries, it's easy to feel taken advantage of or overwhelmed by constant work demands. Establishing limits on your time and energy allows you to preserve your mental and physical health while still being productive and effective in your professional role.

Moreover, boundaries are not just about limiting work; they also ensure that you give your personal life the attention it deserves. Whether it's spending time with family, pursuing hobbies, or simply relaxing, boundaries help you maintain a well-rounded life that goes beyond your job title.

## 1.2 How to Set Boundaries with Your Employer

Setting boundaries with your employer can be challenging, especially in those industries where the expectation is often to be available 24/7. However, it's important to remember that setting boundaries is a form of self-care, and most employers will respect boundaries if communicated clearly and professionally.

- **Communicate your working hours:** Make it clear to your employer what your working hours are, and stick to them. Let them know that while you are dedicated to your work during these hours, you need time outside of work to recharge.
- **Negotiate flexibility:** If your workload is consistently overwhelming, discuss options for flexibility, such as adjusting deadlines, delegating tasks, or working remotely when necessary.
- **Take your time off:** Use your vacation days, sick days, and breaks. Many employees feel guilty about taking time off, but these breaks are essential for maintaining your mental health and preventing burnout.
- **Say no when necessary:** It's important to learn how to say no to additional responsibilities if they will push you beyond your capacity. Politely explain that you're unable to take on more work at the moment due to existing commitments.

### 1.3 How to Set Boundaries with Colleagues

In addition to setting boundaries with your employer, it's important to set boundaries with your colleagues. This can be especially difficult if you work in a collaborative or team-based environment, where colleagues may expect constant communication or immediate responses.

- **Limit after-hours communication:** Politely but firmly let your colleagues know that you won't be responding to work-related messages after a certain time. Encourage them to respect your boundaries by doing the same.

- **Set expectations for meetings:** If meetings are eating into your productive time or personal time, suggest changes to the scheduling or format of meetings. For example, request that meetings be scheduled only during core work hours or held in a more efficient, time-conscious manner.
- **Be clear about your workload:** If a colleague tries to delegate additional tasks to you, be honest about your capacity. Explain that you are currently focused on other priorities and that you'll help when you're able to, or suggest someone else who may have more availability.

## 1.4 How to Set Boundaries with Yourself

Setting boundaries with yourself is just as important as setting them with others. Often, we push ourselves too hard because of internal pressures, such as the desire to succeed, fear of failure, or perfectionism.

- **Stick to your work hours:** Even if no one is pressuring you to work late, it's important to respect your own work hours and not overextend yourself. Avoid checking emails or working on projects during your personal time.
- **Avoid multitasking:** Multitasking can make it difficult to maintain focus and can increase stress. Instead, try to focus on one task at a time and give yourself permission to take breaks between tasks.
- **Prioritize self-care:** Make self-care a non-negotiable part of your daily routine. This includes physical care (such as exercise and nutrition) and mental care (such as relaxation and mindfulness).

- **Recognize when you need a break:** It's essential to be self-aware enough to recognize when you're pushing yourself too hard. If you're feeling overwhelmed, give yourself permission to step back and recharge.

## Section 2: The Role of Self-Awareness: Reflecting on Your Emotional State and Knowing When You Need a Break

Self-awareness is a key factor in maintaining mental health in the workplace. It allows you to monitor your emotional state, recognize signs of stress or burnout, and take proactive steps to address them before they escalate.

### 2.1 What Is Self-Awareness?

Self-awareness is the ability to recognize and understand your own emotions, thoughts, and behaviors. In the context of work-life balance, self-awareness means being attuned to your mental and emotional well-being and understanding how your work environment affects you.

Without self-awareness, it's easy to become disconnected from your own needs, pushing yourself to the brink of exhaustion before realizing that something is wrong. Self-awareness helps you identify when you're feeling stressed, anxious, or overwhelmed, allowing you to take steps to address these feelings before they lead to burnout.

### 2.2 How to Develop Self-Awareness

Developing self-awareness is an ongoing process that requires intentional reflection and mindfulness.

Some strategies to help develop self-awareness include:

- **Regular reflection:** Set aside time each day to reflect on how you're feeling. Are you feeling energized and motivated, or are you feeling stressed and fatigued? Journaling or talking to a trusted friend can help you process your emotions and identify patterns in your mental health.
- **Mindfulness practices:** Mindfulness techniques such as meditation, deep breathing, and progressive muscle relaxation can help you stay present and attuned to your emotions. These practices encourage you to observe your thoughts and feelings without judgment, helping you recognize when something feels off.
- **Track your energy levels:** Pay attention to when you feel most productive and when you feel drained. Are there certain tasks, meetings, or interactions that consistently leave you feeling exhausted? Use this information to adjust your work schedule or seek support when needed.
- **Listen to your body:** Physical symptoms such as headaches, muscle tension, or digestive issues can be signs that you're experiencing too much stress. Tune into your body's signals and take breaks or adjust your workload accordingly.

### 2.3 Knowing When You Need a Break

It's not always easy to recognize when you need a break, especially if you're used to pushing through stress. However, taking regular breaks is essential for maintaining your mental health and productivity. Some signs that you may need a break include:

- **Increased irritability or frustration:** If small annoyances are making you feel disproportionately angry or frustrated, it may be a sign that you need some time away from work.
- **Difficulty concentrating:** If you're having trouble focusing on tasks or find your mind wandering, it could be a sign that your brain needs a rest.
- **Feeling disconnected or apathetic:** If you're feeling disengaged from your work or personal life, it may be a sign that stress is taking a toll on your mental health.
- **Physical symptoms of stress:** If you're experiencing physical symptoms such as headaches, fatigue, or muscle tension, it's a clear sign that your body is under stress and needs a break.

## Section 3: Creating a Balanced Routine: Tips for Developing a Daily Routine That Prioritizes Both Work and Personal Life

A well-structured daily routine can help you balance your work and personal life, ensuring that both areas of your life receive the attention they deserve. However, creating a balanced routine requires intentional planning and self-discipline.

### 3.1 Why Routines Are Important for Work-Life Balance

Routines provide structure and predictability, helping you manage your time effectively and reduce stress. When you have a clear routine, you're less likely to feel overwhelmed by your responsibilities, and you're more likely to prioritize activities that support your mental and physical well-being.

A balanced routine ensures that you allocate time for both work and personal activities. This helps prevent overworking and encourages you to engage in self-care, relaxation, and social activities that support your overall well-being.

### 3.2 Steps to Create a Balanced Routine

- **Define your priorities:** Start by identifying what's most important to you in both your work and personal life. What are your key responsibilities at work? What personal activities bring you joy and fulfillment? Use these priorities to guide your daily routine.
- **Set specific work hours:** Establish clear work hours and stick to them. Avoid working late into the night or on weekends unless absolutely necessary. Having defined work hours helps you maintain a separation between work and personal life.
- **Schedule time for self-care:** Make self-care a regular part of your routine. Whether it's exercise, meditation, or spending time with loved ones, schedule these activities just as you would schedule a work meeting.
- **Take regular breaks:** Incorporate short breaks throughout your workday to prevent burnout and maintain focus. A five-minute break every hour can do wonders for your productivity and mental health.
- **Limit distractions:** Set boundaries with your phone, social media, and other distractions that can disrupt your routine. Focus on one task at a time and avoid multitasking, which can increase stress and reduce efficiency.

### 3.3 Adjusting Your Routine as Needed

It's important to recognize that your routine may need to change over time as your responsibilities and priorities shift. Be flexible and willing to adjust your routine as needed to accommodate new challenges or opportunities.

## Section 4: Work-Life Balance for Different Career Stages: How to Manage Balance at Different Points in Your Career

Work-life balance looks different depending on where you are in your career. What works for someone just starting out may not work for someone in a leadership role. Understanding how to adapt your approach to work-life balance throughout your career can help you maintain mental health and job satisfaction.

### 4.1 Entry-Level Roles

For individuals in entry-level roles, the pressure to prove oneself can make it difficult to maintain a work-life balance. Many young professionals feel the need to work long hours, take on additional responsibilities, or be constantly available in order to advance their careers.

**Tips for Entry-Level Employees:**

- **Set boundaries early on:** Establish clear expectations with your employer about your working hours and availability.
- **Focus on quality over quantity:** Demonstrate your value through the quality of your work rather than the number of hours you put in.

- **Invest in self-development:** While it's important to work hard, don't forget to invest in your personal and professional development outside of work.

### 4.2 Mid-Career Professionals

Mid-career professionals often face different challenges, such as balancing work with family responsibilities or navigating career transitions. At this stage, the demands of work and life can feel overwhelming, making it even more important to prioritize balance.

**Tips for Mid-Career Professionals:**

- **Delegate when possible:** As you progress in your career, learn to delegate tasks to free up time for higher-priority work and personal activities.
- **Seek mentorship:** A mentor can provide valuable guidance on how to navigate work-life balance at this stage of your career.
- **Focus on long-term goals:** While day-to-day tasks are important, keep an eye on your long-term career and personal goals to ensure that your efforts align with your priorities.

### 4.3 Leadership Roles

Leaders often face the challenge of managing not only their own work-life balance but also the well-being of their teams. The pressure to lead by example, meet organizational goals, and support employees can make it difficult for leaders to prioritize their own mental health.

**Tips for Leaders:**

- Model work-life balance for your team. Encourage your employees to set boundaries and take breaks by doing the same yourself.
- Practice delegation and trust. Delegate responsibilities to your team and trust them to handle their tasks, freeing up time for strategic thinking and personal well-being.
- Make time for self-reflection. Regularly assess your own mental health and well-being, and take steps to address any imbalances before they affect your leadership abilities.

## Conclusion:

Finding balance in today's fast-paced work environment requires intentional effort, self-awareness, and a commitment to setting boundaries. By understanding the importance of boundaries, developing self-awareness, creating a balanced routine, and adapting to the different stages of your career, you can prioritize your mental health while still achieving professional success.

# CHAPTER 4

# THE IMPACT OF BURNOUT: HOW TO RECOGNIZE AND PREVENT IT

Burnout has become a pervasive issue in today's breakneck, high-demand work environments. It is characterized by chronic stress, emotional exhaustion, and a sense of detachment from work, often leading to reduced productivity and, in severe cases, long-term mental health issues. Burnout is not just a fleeting moment of frustration or fatigue–it's a serious condition that affects both mental and physical health, relationships, and overall quality of life.

The term burnout was first coined by psychologist Herbert Freudenberger in the 1970s, primarily to describe the condition experienced by healthcare workers under chronic stress. However, burnout has since become a recognized issue across various industries and professions. As the boundaries between work and personal life blur, particularly with remote work and the "always-on" digital culture, burnout is increasingly affecting individuals from all walks of life.

This chapter will delve into the causes, signs, and stages of burnout, exploring its far-reaching impact on mental and physical health. It will also provide actionable strategies for recognizing burnout early, preventing its onset, and recovering from it.

## Section 1: Defining Burnout

### 1.1 What is Burnout?

Burnout is a state of emotional, physical, and mental exhaustion caused by excessive and prolonged stress. It occurs when you feel overwhelmed, emotionally drained, and unable to meet the constant demands of work or life. Over time, burnout can lead to reduced productivity and a loss of interest in work, and it can spill over into other areas of life, affecting your personal relationships and overall well-being.

**Key characteristics of burnout:**

- **Emotional Exhaustion:** Feeling completely drained and depleted of emotional resources. This can manifest as a lack of motivation, energy, and enthusiasm for work or other activities.
- **Depersonalization or Cynicism:** Developing a detached or negative attitude toward work, colleagues, or clients. Burnout can make individuals feel disconnected from their work, often leading to cynicism and irritability.
- **Reduced Personal Accomplishment:** A sense of failure and decreased effectiveness at work, often accompanied by feelings of inadequacy, self-doubt, or a lack of achievement.

Burnout is distinct from regular work stress because it involves a sustained sense of emotional and physical collapse. While short-term stress can be manageable and sometimes even productive, burnout is the result of chronic, unrelenting pressure without adequate recovery time.

## 1.2 The Three Dimensions of Burnout

According to a pioneering researcher in burnout, the condition consists of three core dimensions: emotional exhaustion, depersonalization, and reduced personal accomplishment. Understanding these dimensions can help individuals recognize burnout in themselves or others and take appropriate steps to address it.

- **Emotional Exhaustion:** This is the central aspect of burnout, where individuals feel drained by their work. It is more than just being tired after a long day; it's a constant state of fatigue that doesn't go away even after rest. Emotional exhaustion leaves individuals feeling like they have nothing left to give and makes it difficult to cope with work demands.
- **Depersonalization:** This refers to a sense of detachment or disconnection from work. Individuals may begin to feel cynical, negative, or indifferent about their job, colleagues, or clients. They may also adopt a more impersonal or robotic approach to their tasks, treating work as something they "just get through" rather than something meaningful or rewarding.
- **Reduced Personal Accomplishment:** Burnout leads to a diminished sense of achievement. Individuals may feel that no matter how hard they work, they're not accomplishing anything meaningful. This can result in feelings of incompetence, self-doubt, and frustration.

These three dimensions often interact with and reinforce each other. For instance, emotional exhaustion can lead to depersonalization, and feeling disconnected from work can result in reduced personal accomplishment, creating a vicious cycle that perpetuates burnout.

## Section 2: The Causes of Burnout

Burnout doesn't happen overnight–it develops over time, usually as a result of chronic stress from various sources. Understanding the root causes of burnout is key to preventing it.

### 2.1 Work-Related Causes of Burnout:

Workplace factors are one of the primary contributors to burnout. High demands, long hours, and poor work-life balance can significantly increase the risk of burnout. Some specific work-related causes include:

- **Work Overload:** Consistently high workloads and tight deadlines can overwhelm employees, leaving them feeling constantly behind. When individuals are expected to do more than is feasible within their available time, stress builds up, eventually leading to burnout.
- **Lack of Control:** Employees who feel they have little control over their work–whether in terms of decision-making, scheduling, or task prioritization–are more likely to experience burnout. A lack of autonomy can make people feel powerless and demotivated.
- **Unclear Job Expectations:** When employees aren't sure what is expected of them, it creates confusion and anxiety. Vague job descriptions,

changing priorities, or inconsistent feedback can leave workers feeling uncertain about their performance, which adds to stress.

- **Poor Work-Life Balance:** When work begins to encroach on personal time, it can lead to burnout. Employees who are expected to be "on call" after hours or who regularly work overtime without sufficient breaks may feel that their personal life is being sacrificed for their job.
- **Lack of Social Support:** Employees who feel isolated at work or who lack support from colleagues and supervisors are at higher risk of burnout. Positive social interactions and a supportive workplace culture are essential for buffering against the negative effects of stress.
- **Inadequate Rewards or Recognition:** Employees who feel that their efforts go unrecognized or unrewarded are more likely to burn out. When hard work is not acknowledged, it can lead to feelings of frustration and a loss of motivation.

## 2.2 Personal Factors that Contribute to Burnout

While workplace conditions are a significant contributor, personal factors also play a role in burnout. Certain personality traits and lifestyle choices can increase vulnerability to burnout:

- **Perfectionism:** Individuals who hold themselves to impossibly high standards are more likely to burn out. Perfectionists often struggle with delegation and may take on too much work because they believe only they can do it "correctly." This can lead to chronic stress and exhaustion.

- **People-Pleasing:** Those who have difficulty saying "no" are more likely to take on additional responsibilities, even when they're already overwhelmed. The fear of disappointing others can lead to over commitment and, eventually, burnout.
- **Workaholism:** Some individuals have an intrinsic drive to work excessively, often to the detriment of their health and personal life. This obsessive need to work can prevent proper rest and recovery, increasing the risk of burnout.
- **Lack of Self-Care:** Individuals who neglect self-care—whether through poor sleep habits, lack of exercise, or inadequate relaxation time—are more susceptible to burnout. Self-care is essential for replenishing energy and maintaining resilience in the face of stress.
- **Cultural and Systemic Causes of Burnout:** Beyond individual and workplace factors, there are broader cultural and systemic contributors to burnout:
- **The "Hustle" Culture:** Society often glorifies overworking and the constant pursuit of success, with slogans like "sleep is for the weak" or "grind now, rest later." This pressure to constantly be productive can create a culture where burnout is normalized.
- **Economic Pressures:** In many industries, economic pressures such as job insecurity, layoffs, or reduced benefits force employees to work harder and longer hours to prove their value. This constant pressure to perform can lead to chronic stress and burnout.

- **Technological Overload:** The rise of technology has blurred the boundaries between work and personal life. With smartphones, laptops, and email always within reach, employees are expected to be available at all times, making it difficult to truly disconnect from work.

## Section 3: Recognizing the Signs and Symptoms of Burnout

Burnout doesn't appear suddenly–it develops gradually over time. By recognizing the early warning signs, individuals can take action before burnout fully takes hold.

- **Emotional Symptoms Chronic Fatigue:** Feeling tired all the time, even after a full night's sleep, is one of the most common signs of burnout. This exhaustion often goes beyond physical tiredness, extending to emotional depletion as well.
- **Irritability or Anger:** Burnout can cause individuals to become easily frustrated or short-tempered, even over minor issues. This irritability can strain relationships both at work and in personal life.
- **Feeling Overwhelmed:** Tasks that once seemed manageable may now feel insurmountable. Burnout can lead to a constant sense of being overwhelmed, as if there's never enough time or energy to complete everything.
- **Loss of Motivation:** Individuals experiencing burnout often lose their passion and enthusiasm for work. Tasks that once brought satisfaction or pride may now feel meaningless or burdensome.

- **Depersonalization:** Individuals may begin to feel disconnected from their work, colleagues, or clients. This detachment can manifest as a lack of empathy, cynicism, or apathy.
- **Physical Symptoms Frequent Illness:** Burnout can weaken the immune system, making individuals more susceptible to colds, flu, or other illnesses.
- **Sleep Disturbances:** Insomnia or restless sleep is common among those experiencing burnout. Despite feeling exhausted.

## Section 4: Prevention from Burnout

Burnout is a serious issue that affects both personal well-being and professional productivity. The good news is that burnout can be prevented if addressed early. By adopting proactive strategies that focus on self-care, work-life balance, and emotional well-being, individuals can significantly reduce their risk of burnout. This section explores various ways to prevent burnout, emphasizing both organizational changes and personal actions that promote mental health and sustainability at work.

### 4.1 Establishing a Healthy Work-Life Balance

A poor balance between work and personal life is one of the most common causes of burnout. Many people struggle to maintain boundaries between these two aspects of their lives, especially with the rise of remote work and constant connectivity through digital devices. To prevent burnout, it's crucial to create and protect boundaries that allow time for relaxation, hobbies, and relationships outside of work.

## 4.2 Strategies for Building Work-Life Balance:

**Set Clear Boundaries:** Establish specific work hours, and avoid answering emails or working outside those hours unless absolutely necessary. Communicate these boundaries with colleagues and supervisors to manage expectations.

**4.3 Use Time Management Techniques:** Implement strategies like time-blocking, the Pomodoro Technique, or prioritization frameworks (like the Eisenhower Matrix) to organize your day and ensure you have time for both work tasks and personal activities.

- **Take Regular Breaks:** Studies show that regular short breaks throughout the day improve concentration and reduce stress. A 10- to 15-minute break every 90 minutes can help you stay refreshed and focused.
- **Schedule Personal Time:** Just as you schedule meetings or work deadlines, schedule time for personal activities that help you recharge. This could include exercise, spending time with loved ones, or pursuing hobbies.

## Section 5: Prioritizing Self-Care

Self-care is essential for preventing burnout because it helps you maintain physical, emotional, and mental resilience. When you're taking care of yourself, you are better equipped to handle stress, meet challenges at work, and maintain a positive attitude.

**5.1 Self-Care Strategies:** Sleep Hygiene: Ensure that you get enough sleep each night (7-9 hours for most adults). Establish a bedtime routine, minimize screen time before bed, and create a relaxing environment that supports restful sleep.

- **Exercise:** Physical activity is one of the most effective ways to combat stress and prevent burnout. Exercise boosts endorphins, improves mood, and promotes better sleep. Even short daily activities, like a 30-minute walk, can have a significant positive impact.
- **Nutrition:** A balanced diet is essential for maintaining energy levels and mental clarity. Eating regular meals that include fruits, vegetables, lean proteins, and whole grains can improve focus and reduce fatigue.

**5.2 Mindfulness and Relaxation Techniques:**

Practices such as meditation, deep breathing, or yoga can help reduce stress and promote relaxation. Regular mindfulness practice helps you stay grounded in the present moment, which can reduce anxiety and prevent emotional exhaustion.

- **Hobbies and Leisure:** Engage in activities outside of work that bring you joy and fulfillment. Whether it's reading, painting, gardening, or playing a musical instrument, hobbies provide an outlet for stress and a way to recharge.

## Section 6: Cultivating Emotional Intelligence and Self-Awareness

One of the key ways to prevent burnout is to develop emotional intelligence and self-awareness. By recognizing your emotional state and stress levels, you can take action before burnout takes hold. Emotional intelligence involves the ability to recognize, understand, and manage your own emotions, as well as the ability to empathize with and respond to the emotions of others.

**6.1 Building Emotional Intelligence:** Self-Reflection: Regularly reflect on your emotional state and stress levels. Journaling can be a helpful tool to process emotions and identify stressors. Ask yourself questions such as: "How am I feeling today?" or "What is causing me the most stress?"

- **Recognize Early Warning Signs:** Pay attention to the early signs of burnout, such as irritability, chronic fatigue, or detachment from work. The earlier you recognize these signs, the easier it is to intervene and prevent full-blown burnout.
- **Set Realistic Expectations:** Manage your own expectations about what you can accomplish in a given time frame. Overcommitting and setting unrealistic goals can lead to burnout. Instead, focus on what is achievable, and give yourself permission to slow down when needed.
- **Develop Healthy Emotional Coping Mechanisms:** Instead of turning to unhealthy habits (like overeating, alcohol, or avoidance), develop healthy ways to cope with stress, such as talking to

a friend, practicing relaxation techniques, or engaging in creative outlets.

## 6.2 Building Supportive Relationships and Seeking Help

Burnout often thrives in isolation. Having a strong support system at work and in your personal life can act as a buffer against stress. Whether it's friends, family, or colleagues, sharing your experiences with others can alleviate the emotional burden of burnout.

➢ **Developing a Support System:**

- **Build Strong Workplace Relationships:** Positive relationships with colleagues and supervisors can reduce feelings of isolation and increase job satisfaction. Don't hesitate to reach out to coworkers for support, whether it's for advice, feedback, or simply to share a laugh during a stressful day.
- **Seek Mentorship:** A mentor can provide guidance, offer new perspectives on work-related challenges, and help you navigate stressful situations. Mentorship fosters a sense of belonging and professional growth, which can reduce burnout.
- **Talk to a Professional:** If you're feeling overwhelmed or on the verge of burnout, consider speaking with a mental health professional. Therapists or counsellors can provide valuable coping strategies and help you work through stressors in a constructive way.

- **Join a Support Group:** If you feel isolated, joining a support group (either in person or online) can help you connect with others who are going through similar experiences. Support groups provide a space to share challenges and solutions, helping you feel less alone.

## Section 7: Developing Resilience:

Resilience is the ability to adapt to stress and bounce back from challenges. Building resilience can help prevent burnout by giving you the tools to cope with adversity in a healthy way. While resilience doesn't eliminate stress, it does help you manage it more effectively.

### 7.1 Ways to Build Resilience:

- **Focus on What You Can Control:** Burnout often results from feeling powerless over your circumstances. Instead of dwelling on what you can't change, focus on what you can control–your mindset, your reactions, and the small steps you can take to improve your situation.
- **Cultivate a Growth Mindset:** Embrace the belief that you can learn and grow from challenges. When you encounter setbacks, view them as opportunities for growth rather than as personal failures. This mindset helps reduce the feelings of helplessness that contribute to burnout.
- **Practice Gratitude:** Regularly reflect on what you are grateful for. Research shows that practicing gratitude can improve mental well-being and resilience by shifting your focus from what's going wrong to what's going right.

- **Learn to Adapt to Change:** Flexibility is a key component of resilience. Learning to adapt to changing circumstances—whether it's a shift in work responsibilities or an unexpected personal challenge—will help you navigate stress more effectively.

## 7.2 Addressing Workplace Culture and Organizational Changes

While individual actions are important for preventing burnout, organizations also play a critical role. Workplace culture and organizational practices can either contribute to burnout or help prevent it. Companies that prioritize employee well-being create environments where burnout is less likely to occur.

### Promoting a Healthy Workplace Culture:

- **Encourage Open Communication:** Employers should foster an environment where employees feel comfortable discussing workload challenges, stress, or burnout without fear of judgment. Managers should check in regularly with their teams to address concerns before they escalate.
- **Offer Flexibility:** Providing flexible work options, such as remote work or flexible hours, can help employees manage their work-life balance. Flexibility reduces stress by giving employees more control over their schedules.
- **Provide Mental Health Resources:** Employers can play a proactive role in preventing burnout by offering resources such as counseling services, mental health days, or wellness programs. These

resources signal that the company values employee well-being and mental health.

- **Encourage Breaks and Vacation Time:** Employers should actively encourage employees to take breaks, use their vacation days, and disconnect from work. This helps employees recharge and reduces the likelihood of burnout.
- **Promote a Culture of Recognition:** Recognition and appreciation are key to maintaining employee motivation and morale. Regularly recognizing employees' hard work and contributions can boost their sense of accomplishment and reduce feelings of burnout.

## Section 8: Managing Expectations and Reducing Overload

One of the main causes of burnout is feeling overwhelmed by the sheer volume of work. Learning how to manage expectations—both from yourself and others—is essential for preventing burnout. It's important to communicate openly about your workload and set realistic expectations about what you can accomplish.

### 8.1 Managing Workload and Expectations:

- **Delegate Tasks:** If you're feeling overwhelmed, delegate tasks when possible. This not only lightens your load but also gives colleagues the opportunity to grow by taking on new responsibilities.
- **Negotiate Deadlines:** If you have multiple projects or tight deadlines, negotiate with your supervisor to prioritize tasks. Be honest about

what can be realistically achieved within the given time frame.

- **Learn to Say No:** Saying no to additional responsibilities when your plate is already full is an important skill in preventing burnout. Politely decline tasks or projects that will push you beyond your capacity.

## Conclusion: Taking Proactive Steps to Prevent Burnout

Burnout is a serious condition, but it can be prevented by taking proactive steps to protect your mental and physical health. Prioritizing work-life balance, practicing self-care, building emotional resilience, and fostering supportive relationships are all essential in preventing

# CHAPTER 5

# BUILDING RESILIENCE: MENTAL TOUGHNESS IN THE FACE OF STRESS

In today's hasty, high-pressure world, stress is unavoidable. Whether stemming from work, personal challenges, or societal issues, everyone faces stressors at some point in life. What differentiates those who thrive from those who crumble under pressure is **resilience**–also known as mental toughness.

Resilience is the capacity to recover quickly from difficulties, adapt to challenging circumstances, and maintain psychological well-being in the face of adversity. Mental toughness complements resilience by involving the strength to endure hardship while maintaining focus, persistence, and a positive mindset. This chapter will explore the importance of building resilience, practical techniques for fostering mental toughness, and the benefits of resilience in everyday life.

## Section 1: Defining Resilience and Mental Toughness

### 1.1 What is Resilience?

Resilience is the ability to bounce back from adversity. It doesn't mean avoiding stress or challenges but refers to how we handle those situations when they arise. Resilient individuals can face setbacks, stress, or trauma without losing their sense of purpose or becoming overwhelmed.

Resilience is not a static trait; it can be cultivated and strengthened over time.

**The Key Components of Resilience:**

- **Emotional Regulation:** The ability to manage emotions, particularly during times of stress, without reacting impulsively.
- **Optimism:** Resilient people maintain a positive outlook, even in difficult circumstances, focusing on possibilities rather than limitations.
- **Cognitive Flexibility:** Being able to adapt to changing situations and reframe challenges as opportunities for growth.
- **Social Support:** Resilience often relies on strong personal and professional networks for emotional and practical support.
- **Self-Efficacy:** The belief in one's ability to overcome difficulties and achieve goals. This sense of competence empowers individuals to persevere through challenges.

## Section 2: What is Mental Toughness?

Mental toughness refers to the ability to stay focused and composed under pressure, displaying grit, persistence, and determination in the face of adversity. Unlike resilience, which emphasizes recovery, mental toughness is more about endurance and the ability to withstand stress over extended periods.

## 2.1 The Four C's of Mental Toughness:

- **Control:** Maintaining a sense of control over emotions and situations, rather than being overwhelmed by them.
- **Commitment:** A strong commitment to goals and the determination to see things through, even when obstacles arise.
- **Challenge:** Viewing challenges as opportunities for growth rather than threats to one's success.
- **Confidence:** Believing in oneself and one's abilities, even in the face of setbacks or criticism.

## 2.2 The Importance of Building Resilience

### Why Resilience Matters?

Building resilience is essential because it enables individuals to handle stress, adversity, and change without experiencing long-term psychological harm. Resilience acts as a protective factor against mental health issues such as anxiety, depression, and burnout. Individuals with high resilience are better able to cope with life's inevitable difficulties and can recover more quickly from negative events.

## 2.3 The Benefits of Resilience:

- **Improved Mental Health:** Resilience is strongly associated with lower levels of stress, anxiety, and depression. Resilient individuals are better equipped to handle stress without it negatively impacting their mental well-being.
- **Increased Job Performance:** In the workplace, resilient employees are more likely to stay

productive during challenging times, maintain focus, and find creative solutions to problems.

- **Better Relationships:** Resilient individuals tend to have stronger, healthier relationships. They are more likely to communicate effectively during conflicts and support others during difficult times.
- **Enhanced Problem-Solving Skills:** Resilience fosters a solution-oriented mindset, encouraging individuals to face challenges head-on rather than avoid them.
- **Greater Life Satisfaction:** People who are resilient often report higher overall life satisfaction. They are better able to find meaning and purpose, even in challenging situations.

## 2.4 Mental Toughness in Everyday Life

Mental toughness is not just for athletes or soldiers. It applies to anyone who faces challenges, whether at work, home, or in personal endeavors. Everyday situations that require mental toughness include:

- **Work Stress:** Meeting deadlines, handling difficult colleagues, or navigating corporate politics.
- **Personal Challenges:** Facing illness, financial difficulties, or personal loss.
- **Pursuing Long-Term Goals:** Whether it's advancing in a career, achieving fitness goals, or learning new skills, mental toughness is necessary to stay the course and push through obstacles.

## Section 3: Factors That Influence Resilience and Mental Toughness

### 3.1 Genetic and Environmental Influences:

Resilience is a combination of genetic, psychological, and environmental factors. Some people may be naturally more resilient due to their temperament or personality traits, but resilience is also shaped by life experiences and relationships.

**Key Factors that Shape Resilience:**

- **Genetics:** Studies suggest that some individuals are genetically predisposed to resilience due to their ability to regulate stress hormones more effectively.
- **Upbringing:** Childhood experiences, including a supportive family environment, exposure to adversity, and early opportunities to develop problem-solving skills, can influence an individual's level of resilience.
- **Cultural Factors:** Societal and cultural values around work, perseverance, and community support can either promote or hinder resilience.
- **Education and Socioeconomic Status:** Access to resources, educational opportunities, and social capital can provide the tools necessary for developing resilience.

### 3.2 Personality Traits Associated with Resilience:

- **Hardiness:** A personality trait characterized by a sense of control, commitment, and challenge.

- **Emotional Stability:** The ability to remain calm under pressure and not be easily overwhelmed by emotions.
- **Extra-version:** Extroverts may be more resilient due to their ability to seek social support and view challenges as opportunities.

## Section 4: Strategies for Building Resilience and Mental Toughness

### 4.1 Developing a Positive Mindset

Resilience begins with mindset. A positive, growth-oriented mindset can help you view challenges as opportunities rather than threats. Developing optimism and reframing negative situations can significantly enhance resilience.

**Steps to Cultivate a Positive Mindset:**

- **Practice Gratitude:** Regularly reflect on what you are thankful for. This shifts your focus from problems to positive aspects of your life.
- **Challenge Negative Thoughts:** Replace self-defeating thoughts with empowering ones. Instead of "I can't do this," tell yourself, "I can handle this challenge one step at a time."
- **Focus on What You Can Control:** Resilient individuals focus on the aspects of a situation they can influence, rather than worrying about what's out of their control.

### 4.2 Strengthening Emotional Regulation

One of the key elements of resilience is the ability to manage emotions, especially under stress. Emotional regulation strategies help you stay calm and composed in high-pressure situations.

**Techniques for Emotional Regulation:**

- **Mindfulness Meditation:** Mindfulness helps individuals stay present and reduce the tendency to ruminate on negative thoughts.
- **Deep Breathing Exercises:** Controlled breathing can calm the nervous system, reducing stress and anxiety.
- **Cognitive Reappraisal:** This involves changing the way you think about a stressful situation. For example, instead of viewing a setback as a failure, see it as a learning opportunity.

## 4.3 Building Strong Social Connections

Social support is a critical component of resilience. Resilient individuals often have strong relationships that provide emotional, practical, and psychological support.

**Ways to Strengthen Social Connections:**

- **Build a Support Network:** Cultivate relationships with people who provide encouragement, constructive feedback, and a listening ear during tough times.
- **Practice Active Listening:** Strengthening relationships involves being fully present and engaged in conversations with others.
- **Seek Out Mentorship:** A mentor can provide valuable guidance, offer different perspectives, and help navigate challenges more effectively.

## 4.4 Developing Problem-Solving Skills

Resilient people are excellent problem-solvers. They approach challenges with a solution-focused mindset and look for creative ways to overcome obstacles.

### Steps for Developing Problem-Solving Skills:

- **Break Problems Down:** When faced with a big challenge, break it down into smaller, more manageable parts.
- **Identify Possible Solutions:** Generate multiple solutions to a problem and evaluate the pros and cons of each.
- **Take Action:** Once a solution has been identified, act on it. Resilience is built through action, not avoidance.

## 4.5 Building Physical and Mental Endurance

Resilience requires both mental and physical strength. Physical health has a significant impact on your ability to handle stress, so taking care of your body is an important part of resilience.

### Physical Strategies for Building Endurance:

- **Exercise Regularly:** Physical activity is proven to reduce stress, boost mood, and improve overall resilience.
- **Sleep Well:** Ensure you are getting adequate, high-quality sleep. Lack of sleep can make it difficult to manage stress and stay mentally tough.
- **Nutrition and Hydration:** A healthy diet rich in nutrients supports brain function, which is

critical for emotional regulation and mental clarity.

### 4.6 Cultivating a Growth Mindset

Individuals with a growth mindset believe that their abilities and intelligence can be developed over time. This belief fuels resilience because it allows people to view challenges as learning opportunities rather than threats.

**Ways to Cultivate a Growth Mindset:**

- **Embrace Challenges:** Instead of avoiding difficult tasks, see them as opportunities to grow and improve.
- **Learn from Criticism:** Rather than taking feedback personally, use it as a tool for growth and improvement.
- **Celebrate Effort, Not Just Success:** Recognize that effort is a key part of the learning process, regardless of the outcome.

## Section 5: The Role of Stress in Building Resilience

### 5.1 Positive Stress vs. Negative Stress

Not all stress is harmful. Positive stress, also known as eustress, can actually enhance resilience by pushing individuals to adapt and grow. Eustress motivates individuals to achieve goals, take on challenges, and improve performance. On the other hand, chronic negative stress, or distress, can deplete resilience and lead to burnout, anxiety, and depression. The key to building resilience is learning how to manage stress effectively and use it to your advantage.

**How Stress Strengthens Resilience:**

- **Stress as a Growth Opportunity:** When handled effectively, stress can lead to personal and professional growth. Overcoming stress helps build confidence, self-efficacy, and problem-solving skills.
- **Building Stress Tolerance:** Gradually exposing yourself to manageable stressors can increase your ability to tolerate more significant challenges over time.
- **Adaptive Stress Responses:** Learning to respond to stress in a healthy way—such as through mindfulness, exercise, or relaxation techniques—can strengthen your resilience to future stressors.

## Conclusion: Embracing Resilience and Mental Toughness

Building resilience and mental toughness is an ongoing process that requires intentional effort. By developing emotional regulation skills, fostering a positive mindset, strengthening social connections, and learning how to manage stress effectively, anyone can enhance their ability to cope with life's challenges. Resilience is not about avoiding difficulties, but about embracing them as opportunities for growth and learning. With time, practice, and persistence, resilience and mental toughness can become powerful tools for navigating an increasingly complex and demanding world.

# CHAPTER 6

# THE ROLE OF EMPLOYERS IN SUPPORTING WORK-LIFE BALANCE

Work-life balance has evolved from being a personal responsibility to becoming a central concern for employers in today's work environment. With the increasing pressure of modern work demands, digital connectivity, and the complexities of life outside of work, many employees struggle to achieve balance. When employers prioritize work-life balance, they foster a healthier, more productive workforce. This chapter explores the role of employers in creating supportive environments that encourage work-life balance and the positive outcomes that result for both organizations and employees.

## Section 1: Why Work-Life Balance is a Shared Responsibility

### 1.1 The Shifting Landscape of Work-Life Balance

Traditionally, work-life balance was seen as an individual's concern, something employees had to manage on their own. However, as industries become more aggressive and competitive, the boundary between work and personal life has blurred. With the rise of remote work, flexible hours, and the "always-on" culture enabled by smartphones and technology, employees often find it difficult to disconnect from work.

In this context, work-life balance is no longer just an individual responsibility but a shared one between employers and employees. Organizations that actively support work-life balance can reduce burnout, increase productivity, and improve job satisfaction. Meanwhile, employees who feel supported in balancing their personal and professional lives tend to be more engaged, loyal, and motivated.

### 1.2 The Business Case for Work-Life Balance

Supporting work-life balance is not just a moral obligation—it's also good for business. Research has shown that when employees maintain a healthy balance between work and life, organizations benefit in several ways:

- **Increased Productivity:** Employees who aren't overstressed or overworked are more efficient and creative.
- **Lower Turnover Rates:** A company that supports work-life balance often has higher employee retention rates, saving costs on recruitment and training.
- **Improved Employee Morale:** A balanced work environment fosters higher morale, which translates to better teamwork, communication, and overall company culture.
- **Reduced Absenteeism:** Overworked employees are more prone to stress-related illnesses. Companies that prioritize balance see fewer instances of absenteeism due to health issues.
- **Attracting Top Talent:** In today's competitive job market, offering work-life balance is a key

differentiator that attracts skilled candidates who value flexibility and personal time.

## Section 2: Creating a Supportive Organizational Culture

### 2.1 Leadership and Management's Role

The culture of an organization is often set by its leadership. Employers and managers play a critical role in establishing and maintaining a culture that supports work-life balance. Leaders who understand the importance of balance can set policies, model behaviors, and create an environment that prioritizes employee well-being.

**Key Strategies for Leaders to Support Work-Life Balance:**

- **Leading by Example:** Leaders who maintain a healthy work-life balance themselves set a positive example for employees. Managers who openly take personal time off, prioritize family, or engage in hobbies signal that it's okay for their teams to do the same.
- **Encouraging Open Communication:** Leaders should foster a culture where employees feel comfortable discussing their challenges in balancing work and personal life. Managers should actively check in with their teams to ensure workloads are manageable.
- **Setting Realistic Expectations:** One of the main contributors to work-life imbalance is unrealistic job demands. Leaders should ensure that employees have clear, achievable goals and

deadlines, preventing excessive overtime or burnout.

## 2.2 Establishing Core Values around Balance

To successfully support work-life balance, employers need to embed it in the core values of their organization. This means developing a work culture that doesn't just tolerate but actively encourages balance. When balance becomes a part of the company's DNA, it becomes easier to implement supportive policies and practices that employees will engage with.

### Core Values to Promote:

- **Flexibility:** Flexibility should be a central value in any organization striving to support balance. This includes flexible work hours, remote work options, and adaptability in accommodating employees' personal needs.
- **Respect for Personal Time:** Employers should demonstrate a genuine respect for employees' time outside of work. This includes not expecting staff to respond to emails or calls after hours and respecting time off.
- **Well-Being:** Prioritizing mental and physical well-being ensures that employees can maintain a balance between their work and life responsibilities. Creating a work culture that supports health initiatives, stress management, and mental wellness is essential.

### 2.3 Training and Awareness Programs

Employers can further support work-life balance by offering training programs that educate employees and managers about the importance of balance, stress management, and strategies for time management. Awareness programs can help prevent burnout, and ongoing education about mental health can equip employees with the tools to manage stress more effectively.

**Types of Training to Implement:**

- **Time Management Workshops:** Employees often struggle with managing workloads efficiently. Time management training can provide practical tools for prioritizing tasks, setting boundaries, and organizing schedules.
- **Mental Health and Wellness Programs:** Offering workshops or seminars on mental health, mindfulness, and wellness initiatives can equip employees to better handle stress and create a balanced life.
- **Burnout Prevention Education:** Educating both employees and managers on the signs of burnout and how to prevent it is crucial. This helps create a culture where recognizing and addressing mental and physical exhaustion is normalized.

## Section 3: Implementing Flexible Work Policies

### 3.1 Remote Work and Telecommuting

One of the most significant shifts in the modern workplace has been the rise of remote work and telecommuting. The COVID-19 pandemic further accelerated this trend, highlighting the feasibility of working from home and creating a more flexible work environment.

Remote work allows employees to manage their time better, reduce commuting stress, and integrate their personal lives with work. Employers who offer remote work options show that they trust their employees to complete their work independently, which fosters a sense of autonomy and flexibility.

**Best Practices for Remote Work:**

- **Providing the Right Tools and Technology:** Employers should ensure that employees have access to the tools and technology necessary to work remotely, including secure communication platforms, reliable internet connections, and ergonomic home office equipment.
- **Clear Communication Protocols:** To prevent misunderstandings and ensure productivity, organizations should establish clear communication protocols. This includes setting expectations for meeting times, response times, and project updates.
- **Fostering a Remote Work Culture:** Employers should promote social connections and team cohesion in remote environments through virtual team-building activities, regular check-ins, and online collaboration tools.

## 3.2 Flexible Scheduling

In addition to remote work, offering flexible scheduling allows employees to create a work routine that aligns with their personal responsibilities. Some employees may work best early in the morning, while others may prefer late afternoons or evenings. Flexibility in work hours can greatly enhance work-life balance by allowing employees to take care of family obligations, pursue hobbies, or engage in personal development.

**Benefits of Flexible Scheduling:**

- **Increased Autonomy:** Employees appreciate having control over their work schedules. Flexibility fosters a sense of trust and autonomy, leading to higher job satisfaction.
- **Better Health and Well-Being:** Flexible schedules allow employees to manage their health more effectively, whether that means exercising in the morning, attending medical appointments, or simply getting adequate rest.
- **Improved Work Performance:** Many employees perform better when they can work during their most productive hours. Flexibility enables employees to optimize their work output, leading to improved performance.

## Section 4: Health and Wellness Initiatives

### 4.1 Mental Health Support

Supporting mental health is a critical component of work-life balance. Employers can take an active role in promoting mental wellness by offering resources and services designed to help employees manage stress, anxiety, and mental health challenges.

**Ways to Support Mental Health:**

- **Employee Assistance Programs (EAPs):** EAPs provide confidential counseling services that employees can access to deal with stress, mental health issues, or personal problems. Offering these services demonstrates that employers care about their staff's well-being.
- **Mental Health Days:** Employers should consider allowing mental health days, where employees can take time off to recharge and focus on their mental well-being without using vacation or sick days.
- **Mindfulness and Meditation Programs:** Offering mindfulness programs or guided meditation sessions can help employees develop stress-management techniques, improve focus, and maintain emotional balance.

## 4.2 Physical Health and Well-Being

Physical health is just as important as mental health in supporting work-life balance. Employers can promote a healthy lifestyle by providing access to fitness resources and encouraging healthy habits.

**Health and Wellness Programs to Consider:**

- **On-Site or Virtual Fitness Classes:** Offering fitness classes, either on-site or through virtual platforms, can encourage employees to stay active and prioritize their physical health.

- **Health Screenings and Wellness Checkups:** Employers can organize regular health screenings and wellness checkups to monitor employees' physical health and provide early intervention for health issues.
- **Healthy Snacks and Meals:** Providing access to healthy snacks in the office or offering meal stipends for remote workers can promote better eating habits.

## Section 5: Supporting Employees Through Life Transitions

### 5.1 Parental Leave and Family Support

One of the most challenging life transitions that employees face is becoming a parent. Employers who provide parental leave, flexible working arrangements, and family-friendly policies help employees manage the demands of both work and family life.

**Family Support Initiatives:**

- **Generous Parental Leave Policies:** Offering paid parental leave for both mothers and fathers helps employees transition into parenthood without worrying about their jobs.
- **Childcare Support:** Providing on-site childcare, childcare subsidies, or partnerships with local childcare providers can reduce stress for working parents and improve their ability to balance work and family life.

- **Flexible Return-to-Work Policies:** Allowing parents to transition back to work gradually or with flexible hours after parental leave can ease the pressure and help them find a sustainable balance.

### 5.2 Elder Care and Caregiver Support

As the population ages, many employees find themselves in the role of caregivers for elderly family members. Employers can support caregivers by offering flexible schedules, remote work options, and caregiver support programs.

**Caregiver Support Programs:**

- **Caregiver Leave:** Offering paid or unpaid leave for employees who need to care for elderly or ill family members can provide much-needed relief during difficult times.
- **Support Groups:** Employers can organize support groups for caregivers, where employees can share experiences, resources, and advice on balancing work and caregiving responsibilities.

## Section 6: Measuring and Enhancing Work-Life Balance Policies

### Conducting Employee Surveys

To understand whether work-life balance policies are effective, employers should regularly survey employees about their experiences and satisfaction with existing programs. Anonymous surveys allow employees to share candid feedback, which can inform improvements in work-life balance initiatives.

### Tracking Employee Well-Being Metrics

Employers can track key metrics such as absenteeism, employee engagement, turnover rates, and job satisfaction to measure the impact of work-life balance policies. Higher engagement and lower turnover rates are often indicative of a balanced work environment.

### Continuous Improvement

Supporting work-life balance is an ongoing effort. Employers must remain adaptable and open to evolving their policies to meet the changing needs of the workforce. Regular feedback, coupled with a commitment to improvement, will ensure that work-life balance initiatives remain effective and relevant.

## Conclusion: Employers as Catalysts for Positive Change

Employers play a pivotal role in shaping the work-life balance of their employees. By creating a supportive organizational culture, offering flexible work policies, and promoting health and wellness, employers can foster a balanced, engaged, and productive workforce. The benefits of supporting work-life balance are clear: happier employees, stronger company loyalty, and improved business outcomes. With the right strategies in place, employers can become catalysts for positive change, helping employees navigate the demands of modern work while leading fulfilling personal lives.

# CHAPTER 7

# PRODUCTIVITY WITHOUT SACRIFICE: WORKING SMARTER, NOT HARDER

In today's digital world, being productive no longer just means working more hours or completing more tasks. The concept of productivity has evolved, particularly as the boundaries between work and personal life have blurred due to technological advancements. Working from home, constant connectivity, and high expectations can easily lead to burnout if not managed properly.

Redefining Productivity involves rethinking how we approach work, with a focus on quality over quantity. It is about achieving maximum results with minimal wasted effort and resources. Instead of pushing yourself to the limit with longer work hours, the aim is to achieve a balance that allows for high performance while also prioritizing well-being.

**Core Concepts to Address:**

- **The difference between being busy and being productive:** Many workers feel overwhelmed with tasks but find themselves accomplishing little of significance. This chapter addresses this distinction and introduces a new approach to achieving more without additional stress.
- **The shift from working harder to working smarter:** The traditional model of success—working long hours, sacrificing sleep, and pushing

through exhaustion—needs to be replaced with smarter strategies that focus on impact.

- **Why mental well-being is critical to productivity:** The pursuit of productivity should not come at the expense of mental health. The goal is to avoid burnout while maximizing output.

## Section 1: Understanding the Difference between Efficiency and Productivity

### 1.1 Defining Efficiency vs. Productivity

Efficiency and productivity are often used interchangeably, but they differ in significant ways. Efficiency refers to the ability to complete tasks with minimal wasted time or resources, while productivity focuses on the meaningful output of work.

- **Efficiency is task-oriented:** For example, sending emails more quickly or automating repetitive tasks.
- **Productivity is results-oriented:** For instance, creating a marketing strategy that drives business growth.

**Examples to Illustrate:**
Imagine an employee who spends eight hours responding to emails and attending meetings. They may appear busy, but their work lacks significant output. Alternatively, another employee spends four hours developing a client proposal and closes a major deal. This second employee has been more productive, despite working fewer hours.

**Productivity Pitfalls:**

- **Multitasking:** While it may seem efficient, multitasking often results in errors, reduced focus, and lower overall productivity. Studies show that switching between tasks can decrease performance by as much as 40%.
- **Working longer hours:** After a certain point, working more hours doesn't equate to higher productivity. The law of diminishing returns applies, where additional hours lead to mental fatigue, slower work, and mistakes.

## 1.2 The Pitfalls of Overwork

Overwork can result in a productivity paradox where the more you work, the less effective you become. Constantly pushing beyond your limits leads to diminished cognitive abilities, affecting creativity, decision-making, and emotional well-being. In turn, this negatively impacts performance.

**Key Consequences of Overwork:**

- **Cognitive decline:** After a certain number of hours, the brain's ability to solve problems and think creatively decreases.
- **Health risks:** Long-term overwork is linked to anxiety, depression, and physical issues like hypertension and insomnia.
- **Diminishing returns:** Employees may appear busy but accomplish less, requiring more time to fix errors or re-do work.
- **Statistics to Support the Case:** Research by the World Health Organization has shown that working 55 hours or more per week increases the

risk of stroke and heart disease. Further studies indicate that employees are most productive working around 35–40 hours per week, with declines in productivity noted as the hours increase beyond this threshold.

## Section 2: The Key to Working Smarter: Prioritization and Focus

### 2.1 The Pareto Principle (80/20 Rule)

The Pareto Principle is one of the most powerful concepts for improving productivity without working harder. This principle suggests that 80% of results come from 20% of efforts, meaning that a small portion of activities leads to the majority of outcomes.

**Practical Application:**

- **Analyze your tasks:** Start by looking at your to-do list and identifying which tasks have the most impact. These are the 20% that drive 80% of your results.
- **Focus on high-value activities:** Prioritize tasks that directly contribute to your goals, such as strategy development, key meetings, or critical projects.
- **Eliminate or minimize low-value tasks:** Tasks such as excessive email management, attending non-essential meetings, and busywork should either be delegated or removed.

**Examples:**

A marketing professional may find that 20% of the social media platforms they use drive 80% of customer engagement. Focusing on these key platforms, instead of spreading efforts thin, would result in better productivity.

## 2.2 Prioritization with the Eisenhower Matrix

The Eisenhower Matrix is another powerful tool for prioritizing tasks based on urgency and importance. It helps you sort your tasks into four categories:

- **Important and Urgent:** Must be done immediately (e.g., crisis management or meeting deadlines).
- **Important but Not Urgent:** Contribute to long-term goals but can be scheduled (e.g., strategic planning or self-development).
- **Urgent but Not Important:** Time-sensitive tasks that can often be delegated (e.g., routine reports or meeting scheduling).
- **Not Important and Not Urgent:** Tasks that can be minimized or eliminated (e.g., unnecessary social media scrolling).

### Practical Application:

At the beginning of each day or week, use the Eisenhower Matrix to categorize your tasks. This practice ensures that you spend the most time on high-impact, important work rather than being bogged down by non-essential activities.

## 2.3 Time Blocking and Deep Work

Time blocking involves scheduling specific blocks of time dedicated to focused work on a single task or project. During these blocks, distractions are minimized, and deep concentration is maintained.

Time blocking is particularly useful for high-priority tasks identified through the Pareto Principle and the Eisenhower Matrix.

Deep work refers to periods of uninterrupted focus on cognitively demanding tasks. Research shows that deep work enhances learning, problem-solving, and creativity, often resulting in higher-quality work in less time.

**Practical Example:**

Set aside two hours every morning for deep work on high-priority tasks. During this time, turn off phone notifications, close unnecessary tabs, and resist the temptation to multitask.

Research Support: A study shows that individuals who engage in deep, focused work sessions outperform their peers who are constantly distracted. A single deep work session can often produce better results than a full day of shallow, unfocused work.

## Section 3: Leveraging Technology to Enhance Productivity

### 3.1 Automation and Delegation

In today's world, technology offers numerous tools that can automate routine tasks, saving time and increasing efficiency. Automation allows you to streamline repetitive tasks like sending follow-up emails, scheduling meetings, or updating reports.

**Examples of Automation Tools:**

- **Email automation:** Use tools like Mailchimp etc. to automate email marketing campaigns.
- **Scheduling automation:** Platforms like Calendly or Doodle etc. can automate meeting scheduling, reducing back-and-forth communication.
- **Project management:** Tools like Trello or Monday allow teams to automate workflows, assign tasks, and track progress without manual follow-ups.

Delegation is another critical component of working smarter. Delegating allows you to focus on high-priority tasks while others handle less critical activities. The key to effective delegation is ensuring that you delegate tasks that others can perform adequately, allowing you to conserve energy for your most impactful work.

**Practical Delegation Tips:**

- **Choose wisely:** Select tasks that don't require your direct involvement, such as routine reports or customer service inquiries.
- **Provide clear instructions:** Set clear expectations for the delegated task, including deadlines and desired outcomes.
- **Follow-up without micromanaging:** Check in periodically to ensure progress, but avoid hovering over the person handling the task.

### 3.2 Using Productivity Tools

There are countless productivity tools available today that can help you stay organized, manage time effectively, and collaborate with others. These tools can drastically reduce the time spent on mundane tasks, allowing you to focus on high-impact work.

**Popular Productivity Tools:**

- **Task Management Tools:**Clickup, Asana, or Notion for tracking tasks and deadlines.
- **Collaboration Tools:** Slack, Zoom, or Google Workspace for seamless communication and document sharing among teams.
- **Time-Tracking Tools:** Toggl or RescueTime to monitor how you're spending your time and identify inefficiencies.

Example: A team of marketing professionals might use Asana to manage project timelines, assign tasks, and track progress in one centralized platform. This prevents the need for endless email threads and helps team members stay aligned.

## Section 4: The Power of Routines and Habits

### 4.1 Building Productive Habits

Productive habits are the backbone of long-term efficiency. Once certain behaviors become habitual, they no longer require conscious thought, which frees up mental energy for more demanding tasks.

**Steps to Build Productive Habits:**

- **Start Small:** Rather than overhauling your routine all at once, focus on small, manageable changes. For example, spend 10 minutes each evening planning your tasks for the next day.
- **Be Consistent:** Habits are built through repetition. Stick to your new routine for at least 21 days to solidify the habit.
- **Use Triggers:** A trigger is something that prompts the habit to begin. For instance, a morning coffee could trigger a review of your day's goals.
- **Reward Yourself:** Reinforce your habit with a reward, such as taking a short break or treating yourself after completing the task.

## 4.2 The Role of Morning Routines

A structured morning routine can set the tone for a productive day. Successful people often attribute their achievements to starting the day with a clear mind and focused plan.

**Elements of a Productive Morning Routine:**

- **Review your goals:** Begin each day by reviewing your goals and priorities. This ensures that your day starts with direction and purpose.
- **Plan your day:** Block out time for your most important tasks and make time for deep work sessions.
- Incorporate self-care: Activities like stretching, meditation, or a healthy breakfast

can boost mental clarity and prepare you for a productive day ahead.

## Section 5: Managing Energy, Not Just Time

### 5.1 The Importance of Energy Management

Managing time is essential, but managing energy is equally important. If you are physically or mentally exhausted, no amount of time management can make you productive. Energy management involves recognizing your body's natural rhythms and aligning your work schedule with periods of peak energy.

**Practical Tips for Managing Energy:**

- **Work with your natural energy cycles:** Identify when you are most alert and productive (e.g., morning or afternoon) and schedule high-priority tasks during these times.
- **Take regular breaks:** Implement the Pomodoro Technique (work for 25 minutes, take a 5-minute break) or work in 90-minute cycles to prevent burnout.
- **Prioritize self-care:** Ensure that you're getting enough sleep, eating nutritious meals, and engaging in physical activity. These habits are essential for maintaining sustained energy throughout the day.

### 5.2 Combating Procrastination

Procrastination is one of the most significant barriers to working smarter. It often occurs when tasks seem overwhelming or when there is a lack of motivation.

However, procrastination can be tackled with the right strategies.

**Tips to Overcome Procrastination:**

- **Break tasks into smaller steps:** Large, complex tasks can feel overwhelming, leading to procrastination. Break them down into smaller, manageable steps to make them feel more achievable.
- **Use deadlines and accountability:** Set clear deadlines for tasks, even if they are self-imposed. Share your goals with a colleague or friend who can hold you accountable.
- **Practice the Two-Minute Rule:** If a task can be done in two minutes or less, do it immediately rather than letting it pile up on your to-do list.

## Conclusion: Mastering Productivity without Sacrifice

To achieve productivity without sacrifice, it's essential to rethink traditional approaches to work. By embracing strategies like prioritization, deep work, and energy management, you can accomplish more in less time while preserving your well-being. Working smarter, not harder, is about leveraging tools, habits, and mindful practices to optimize output without burning out. This chapter provides a blueprint for balancing productivity and self-care, proving that success doesn't have to come at the expense of mental health and happiness.

# CHAPTER 8

# WORK-LIFE INTEGRATION VS. WORK-LIFE BALANCE

The concept of balancing work and personal life has changed dramatically over the years. Once, the lines between work and home were clearly drawn; you went to work, clocked out, and left your job behind until the next day. But with technological advancements and shifts in work culture–such as remote work, freelance opportunities, and the rise of the gig economy–the boundary between work and personal time has blurred. This shift has led to the emergence of work-life integration as an alternative to the traditional work-life balance model.

In today's speedy, hyper-connected world, individuals are exploring new ways to harmonize their professional duties with personal life. As a result, the conversation has evolved beyond simple balance. Work-life balance focuses on separating work from personal life, with the goal of achieving an equal division of time and energy between the two. On the other hand, work-life integration aims to blend work and life in a way that allows both to coexist without rigid boundaries.

This chapter delves into the distinctions between work-life balance and work-life integration. We will explore the benefits, challenges, and practical applications of both approaches, helping you determine which method works best for your circumstances and goals. By understanding the intricacies of each concept, you can tailor a strategy that enhances productivity, maintains mental health, and promotes overall satisfaction in both work and life.

## Section 1: Understanding Work-Life Balance

### 1.1 The Traditional Concept of Work-Life Balance

Work-life balance is rooted in the idea that professional and personal responsibilities are separate domains that should be treated as such. The goal is to divide time, attention, and energy between work and home life in a way that neither overwhelms the other. This approach often involves setting strict boundaries, such as maintaining specific work hours and leaving work-related tasks at the office. The underlying assumption of work-life balance is that keeping work and life distinct promotes mental well-being, reduces stress, and helps individuals avoid burnout. This method works particularly well in traditional work environments where employees have set hours and are not expected to be "on call" outside of those hours.

**Key Principles of Work-Life Balance:**

- **Separation of Work and Life:** Work and personal life are viewed as two separate entities, and boundaries are established to prevent overlap.
- **Time Allocation:** Efforts are made to allocate time evenly between work and personal activities, ensuring that neither aspect dominates.

- **Focus on Rest and Relaxation:** Personal time is spent away from work, engaging in activities that promote mental relaxation and rejuvenation.

### 1.2 Challenges of Maintaining Work-Life Balance

Though the idea of work-life balance is appealing, it is not without its challenges. Achieving a perfect balance can be difficult for a variety of reasons:

- **Increasing Work Demands:** Many professionals, especially those in high-pressure industries, are expected to be available outside of traditional work hours. Emails, phone calls, and urgent requests can intrude on personal time, making it difficult to maintain clear boundaries.
- **Blurred Lines Due to Technology:** The rise of smartphones, laptops, and other mobile devices has made it easier for work to follow employees home. With the constant influx of work-related notifications, it can be hard to "switch off" after hours.
- **Feelings of Guilt and Pressure:** Individuals may feel guilty about prioritizing personal time when work demands are high. This guilt can lead to overwork and burnout, even when the intention is to create balance.
- **Rigid Expectations:** Work-life balance often relies on the idea of equally dividing time between work and personal life. However, this may not always be possible due to the unpredictable nature of work, family emergencies, or personal obligations.

### 1.3 Benefits of Achieving Work-Life Balance

Despite these challenges, work-life balance can offer significant benefits when successfully implemented:

- **Improved Mental Health:** By keeping work and personal life separate, individuals can engage in hobbies, rest, and relaxation during their off time, leading to lower stress levels and improved mental well-being.
- **Increased Productivity:** When individuals have time to recharge, they often return to work more focused and motivated. This leads to higher productivity during work hours, as they are not constantly fatigued.
- **Stronger Relationships:** Clear boundaries between work and personal time allow for deeper connections with family, friends, and loved ones. When individuals are fully present in their personal lives, they are able to strengthen relationships and build meaningful connections.
- **Reduced Burnout:** By dedicating time for self-care and leisure, individuals can avoid the constant cycle of work-related stress that leads to burnout.

## Section 2: What is Work-Life Integration?

### 2.1 The Concept of Work-Life Integration

Unlike work-life balance, which advocates for the clear separation of work and personal life, work-life integration promotes a more fluid approach. In this model, work and life coexist, often overlapping and blending into one another. Rather than viewing work and life as separate domains, work-life integration encourages individuals to think about how they can harmonize these two areas.

For many people, work-life integration is a natural response to the demands of the modern workplace, where technology allows for constant connectivity. In this model, work doesn't need to be confined to traditional office hours, and personal activities don't have to be restricted to evenings or weekends.

**Key Principles of Work-Life Integration:**

- **Flexible Boundaries:** Work and personal tasks are blended together, allowing individuals to handle personal matters during work hours and vice versa. For example, attending a personal appointment during the workday and catching up on work later in the evening.
- **Prioritizing Results:** The focus is on the quality of work completed rather than the time spent working. As long as tasks are accomplished effectively, individuals have the flexibility to manage their time as they see fit.
- **Leveraging Technology:** Modern tools and platforms enable individuals to stay connected and work from anywhere. This flexibility allows for seamless transitions between work and personal life.

## 2.2 Benefits of Work-Life Integration

For those who prefer flexibility and autonomy in managing their time, work-life integration offers several advantages:

- **Increased Flexibility:** Work-life integration allows individuals to structure their day around their personal and professional priorities. For instance, someone might attend a child's school event in the morning and work later in the day to meet a deadline.
- **Enhanced Productivity:** By focusing on outcomes rather than strict hours, employees can achieve more in less time. This approach can also lead to greater job satisfaction, as individuals have more control over their schedules.
- **Adaptability to Modern Work Environments:** With the rise of remote work and the gig economy, work-life integration reflects the reality that many professionals no longer work within traditional hours or in a fixed location.

## 2.3 Challenges of Work-Life Integration

While work-life integration offers flexibility, it can also present challenges:

- **Blurred Boundaries:** Without clear distinctions between work and personal time, individuals may feel like they are always "on," leading to burnout and decreased mental well-being.
- **Difficulty Disconnecting:** Work-life integration can make it difficult to fully disconnect from work, as tasks may spill over into evenings, weekends, and even vacations.
- **Overwork:** In some cases, the blending of work and life can lead to longer hours, as individuals may feel pressure to be available for work at all times, especially in remote work environments.

## Section 3: Work-Life Balance vs. Work-Life Integration: Key Differences

Although work-life balance and work-life integration aim to create harmony between work and personal life, they differ significantly in approach and execution. Below are key distinctions between the two concepts:

### 3.1 Boundaries

- **Work-Life Balance:** Encourages strict boundaries between work and personal life. Individuals strive to maintain separation between the two areas, ensuring that work does not interfere with personal time.
- **Work-Life Integration:** Emphasizes flexible boundaries, with work and personal tasks blending together. Individuals might handle personal matters during work hours and complete work tasks during personal time.

### 3.2 Time Management

- **Work-Life Balance:** Involves dividing time equally between work and personal life. The goal is to allocate specific hours for work and separate time for relaxation, hobbies, or family.
- **Work-Life Integration:** Focuses on managing time based on priorities rather than splitting it equally. Individuals may shift between work and personal activities throughout the day, depending on what is most pressing.

### 3.3 Flexibility

- **Work-Life Balance:** Provides structure and predictability, which can reduce stress for individuals who thrive on routine and boundaries. However, it may not work well for those in dynamic, fast-paced industries.
- **Work-Life Integration:** Offers greater flexibility and adaptability, which can be beneficial for individuals in roles that require constant connectivity or irregular hours.

### 3.4 Impact on Mental Health

- **Work-Life Balance:** Helps individuals avoid burnout by creating clear time for relaxation and recovery. However, strict adherence to balance can cause stress if work intrudes into personal time.
- **Work-Life Integration:** Can reduce stress for those who prefer flexibility, but if not managed carefully, it can lead to overwork and difficulty disconnecting from work, negatively impacting mental health.

## Section 4: Finding What Works for You: Balance, Integration, or a Hybrid Approach

Neither work-life balance nor work-life integration is a one-size-fits-all solution. The right approach depends on personal preferences, professional demands, and individual circumstances. For some, maintaining strict boundaries and adhering to a balanced schedule may provide the structure needed to thrive. For others, the freedom to blend work and life seamlessly may be more conducive to productivity and well-being.

In many cases, a hybrid approach may be the most practical solution. This involves combining elements of both work-life balance and work-life integration, allowing for flexibility when needed while still maintaining some degree of separation between work and personal time.

## 4.1 Assessing Your Needs: Key Considerations

When deciding whether to pursue work-life balance, work-life integration, or a hybrid approach, consider the following factors:

- **Work Environment:** Does your job require you to be constantly available, or can you maintain set hours? If your work is highly demanding, work-life integration may offer more flexibility. If your work allows for routine, work-life balance might be more appropriate.
- **Personal Responsibilities:** Do you have caregiving duties, hobbies, or other commitments that require flexibility? Individuals with complex personal schedules may benefit from work-life integration, while those with more structured personal lives may prefer balance.
- **Mental Health and Well-Being:** How well do you handle stress? If constant connectivity leads to burnout, work-life balance may help protect your mental health. If you find rigidity stressful, work-life integration might reduce pressure and offer greater control.

## Conclusion: Moving Beyond Balance towards Integration

The evolving nature of work has brought new challenges and opportunities for managing professional and personal responsibilities. While work-life balance remains a valuable goal for many, work-life integration offers a flexible alternative that aligns with the demands of modern work environments.

Ultimately, the goal is not to adhere strictly to one model but to create a personalized strategy that supports both professional success and personal fulfillment. By understanding the principles of work-life balance and work-life integration, individuals can make informed choices that lead to healthier, more productive lives.

# CHAPTER 9

# MANAGING PERSONAL RELATIONSHIPS WHILE BALANCING WORK

Balancing a demanding career with the maintenance of personal relationships is one of the greatest challenges faced by modern professionals. With the lines between work and personal life becoming increasingly blurred due to technology, remote work, and the instant nature of modern life, sustaining meaningful personal connections while excelling at work is more complex than ever.

This chapter explores how work-life balance and personal relationships intersect. It delves into strategies to foster and maintain healthy relationships—whether with partners, family members, friends, or colleagues—while navigating the demands of a busy professional life. Through this discussion, we will address common challenges, such as time constraints, communication barriers, and emotional burnout, while offering solutions to preserve intimacy, trust, and connection in personal relationships without compromising professional success.

## Section 1: The Importance of Personal Relationships in a Busy Work Life

### 1.1 The Value of Emotional Support

One of the most significant benefits of nurturing personal relationships is the emotional support they provide. Work can be stressful, and personal relationships serve as a vital source of encouragement, motivation, and emotional grounding. A strong support system helps buffer against stress, promoting mental health and overall well-being.

- Studies show that individuals with strong personal connections are more resilient and experience lower rates of burnout, anxiety, and depression. Knowing that you have people who care about your well-being can significantly reduce the negative impacts of work-related stress.
- Personal relationships also offer perspective. While work can sometimes feel overwhelming, having close relationships helps individuals put professional challenges into context, reminding them of the broader picture and what truly matters.

### 1.2 Impact on Physical Health

Relationships affect not only mental health but also physical health. Having supportive personal relationships has been linked to better immune function, lower blood pressure, and longer lifespans. When work stress is high, these health benefits are even more critical. Relationships encourage self-care, whether it's through emotional support, shared activities, or a positive influence on lifestyle choices.

- Research has shown that those in satisfying relationships tend to experience less stress and better physical health outcomes compared to those who are isolated or experience relationship conflict.

### 1.3 Enhancing Career Success through Strong Relationships

Strong personal relationships can actually contribute to professional success. Supportive partners and family members help individuals maintain the energy and motivation required to perform well at work. Moreover, meaningful personal connections foster a sense of balance, enabling professionals to focus more effectively on their work when they feel secure and fulfilled in their personal lives.

- A partner or close friend who understands the demands of your career can offer invaluable support during tough times, helping you navigate challenges with greater emotional resilience.
- Building healthy relationships outside of work also allows for emotional release and helps prevent work-related stress from spilling over into every aspect of life, thus improving concentration and performance at work.

## Section 2: Common Challenges in Managing Relationships alongside Work

Balancing personal relationships while pursuing career success is not without its challenges. The following are common issues that professionals face:

### 2.1 Time Constraints and Scheduling Conflicts

One of the biggest hurdles in maintaining relationships while working is simply finding enough time to invest in those connections. Long work hours, unpredictable schedules, and the increasing expectation to be available outside of traditional work hours can make it difficult to prioritize relationships.

- **The struggle for time:** Professionals often find themselves caught between long workdays, after-hours emails, and the need to perform tasks during personal time. As a result, relationships may take a back seat, leading to feelings of neglect among loved ones.
- **Lack of quality time:** Even when time is available, the quality of that time may suffer if one is mentally preoccupied with work or too exhausted to engage meaningfully with others.

## 2.2 Emotional Exhaustion and Burnout

Emotional exhaustion from work can seep into personal relationships. When individuals are drained by their professional lives, they may have little energy left for meaningful interactions with family and friends. This emotional burnout can lead to misunderstandings, conflicts, and a general lack of engagement in personal relationships.

- **Signs of emotional burnout:** These include irritability, fatigue, lack of interest in previously enjoyable activities, and difficulty managing emotions. If not addressed, burnout can harm relationships, as partners or loved ones may feel that they are no longer a priority.

### 2.3 Communication Breakdowns

Another challenge professionals face is effective communication. When work takes up most of one's attention, communication with partners, family members, or friends may become rushed, superficial, or inconsistent. Miscommunication and lack of communication can lead to conflicts, misunderstandings, and a feeling of emotional distance in relationships.

- **Communication fatigue:** After a long day of meetings, emails, and work-related discussions, some individuals may feel too mentally tried to engage in deep, meaningful conversations at home. This can lead to emotional disconnects with loved ones, particularly if their communication needs are not met.

### 2.4 Role Confusion and Role Strain

Balancing multiple roles, such as being a spouse, parent, friend, and employee, can be overwhelming. Role strain occurs when the demands of one role conflict with the expectations of another. For example, professionals may feel torn between meeting work deadlines and attending important family events, leading to feelings of guilt or frustration.

- **Role conflict:** Professionals often struggle to meet the expectations of their work and personal lives simultaneously, leading to stress. This can cause strain in relationships, especially if loved ones feel they are being deprioritized.

### 2.5 Guilt and Resentment

Many professionals experience guilt over their inability to spend more time with their loved ones. This guilt can cause them to overcompensate by trying to "make up for lost time" or over-apologizing. Over time, however, this cycle can lead to resentment from partners who may feel their needs are not being met, despite the efforts made.

## Section 3: Strategies for Managing Personal Relationships While Balancing Work

Managing relationships alongside work requires intentional effort, clear communication, and the ability to prioritize both personal and professional responsibilities. The following strategies can help individuals' foster meaningful connections while maintaining a successful career:

### 3.1 Prioritizing Time for Relationships

One of the most effective ways to manage relationships while balancing work is to prioritize time for loved ones. Scheduling dedicated time for family, friends, or partners–just as one would schedule a work meeting–ensures that relationships are not neglected.

- **Calendar management:** Many professionals find success by blocking out time on their calendars specifically for personal activities, whether it's a weekly date night, family dinner, or time with friends. By treating this time as non-negotiable, they ensure that relationships remain a priority.

- **Micro-interactions:** Even during busy periods, small interactions can help maintain connection. A quick text, phone call, or coffee break with a loved one during the day can go a long way in showing that they are valued.

### 3.2 Setting Boundaries with Work

Creating boundaries between work and personal life is essential for maintaining healthy relationships. This can involve setting limits on work-related communication after hours, as well as being clear with colleagues about personal time commitments.

- **No-phone zones:** Designating certain times or places–such as during dinner or while spending time with loved ones–as "no-work zones" can help professionals disconnect from work and be fully present with family and friends.
- **Establishing boundaries at work:** Clearly communicating boundaries with colleagues and supervisors is also key. Professionals who are upfront about their need to prioritize personal time are more likely to have their boundaries respected.

### 3.3 Improving Communication

Open, honest, and consistent communication is crucial for maintaining strong personal relationships. This involves not only sharing personal experiences and feelings but also actively listening and responding to the needs of others.

- **Active listening:** Rather than simply hearing what a partner or loved one is saying, active listening involves being fully engaged in the conversation, showing empathy, and providing thoughtful responses.
- **Sharing work-related stress:** It can be helpful to share work-related stress with loved ones, as long as this does not dominate the conversation. This fosters openness and allows loved ones to understand the pressures professionals face, helping them offer better support.

## 3.4 Balancing Personal and Professional Goals

Achieving a balance between personal and professional goals requires regular reflection and adjustment. Professionals should take time to evaluate whether their work aligns with their values and allows them to prioritize their personal relationships.

- **Periodic self-assessment:** Regularly assessing work-life balance can help individuals identify areas where they may need to make changes. This may involve reassessing work commitments, setting new goals, or redistributing time to ensure that relationships are not being neglected.
- **Creating a personal vision statement:** Professionals can benefit from creating a personal vision statement that outlines their priorities and values. By aligning career decisions with this statement, they can ensure

that their personal relationships remain a priority.

### 3.5 Practicing Self-Care

Self-care is essential for maintaining both personal relationships and professional success. When individuals take care of their mental, emotional, and physical well-being, they are better equipped to manage the demands of work and relationships.

- **Physical well-being:** Regular exercise, healthy eating, and adequate sleep are essential components of self-care that contribute to overall well-being and help reduce stress, which in turn benefits relationships.
- **Emotional well-being:** Mindfulness practices, therapy, or journaling can help individuals process emotions and manage stress more effectively, leading to more meaningful interactions with loved ones.

### 3.6 Seeking Professional Help

For individuals who find it particularly difficult to balance work and personal relationships, seeking professional help from a therapist or counselor can be beneficial. Couples counseling, family therapy, or individual therapy can help address underlying issues and provide tools for better communication and emotional management.

- **Therapeutic interventions:** Therapists can offer strategies for managing stress, improving communication, and finding balance between work and relationships. They can also help individuals navigate role strain and burnout.

## Section 4: The Role of Technology in Balancing Work and Relationships

Technology has both facilitated and complicated the balance between work and personal relationships. While it allows for greater flexibility and connectivity, it can also create a sense of constant availability, making it difficult to separate work from personal life.

### 4.1 Using Technology to Foster Connection

While technology can be a source of distraction, it can also be used to foster connection with loved ones, especially when physical distance is a barrier.

- **Virtual connection:** For professionals who travel frequently or work remotely, video calls, messaging apps, and social media can help maintain personal relationships by providing opportunities for regular communication.
- **Shared activities online:** Many couples and families use technology to engage in shared activities, such as watching movies together, playing online games, or sharing photos and updates.

### 4.2 Limiting Technology Use to Protect Personal Time

While technology can help maintain connections, it is also important to set limits on its use, particularly in relation to work. Professionals should be mindful of how much time they spend on their devices during personal time and take steps to disconnect from work when they are with loved ones.

- **Digital detox:** Scheduling regular breaks from technology, especially during personal interactions, can help individuals be more present with their loved ones. Some professionals set aside time each day to turn off work emails, mute notifications, or leave their devices in another room to focus on personal relationships.

## Conclusion: Balancing Work and Personal Relationships for Lasting Fulfillment

Balancing personal relationships with the demands of a busy work life is a complex but essential task for long-term well-being. Strong relationships provide emotional support, improve mental and physical health, and can even enhance professional success. However, managing these relationships requires intentional effort, clear communication, and setting boundaries to prevent work from overshadowing personal connections.

By prioritizing time for loved ones, improving communication, setting work boundaries, and practicing self-care, professionals can successfully balance their careers with their personal lives. In doing so, they not only maintain meaningful relationships but also enhance their overall happiness and fulfillment.

# CHAPTER 10

# DIGITAL DETOX: MANAGING TECHNOLOGY FOR BETTER MENTAL HEALTH

In today's world, technology is omnipresent, shaping every aspect of our lives—from how we work, communicate, and entertain ourselves to how we relax and manage stress. While the digital age has brought countless benefits, such as instant communication, access to vast amounts of information, and the ability to work remotely, it has also introduced new challenges. For many people, technology has become an all-consuming part of life, leading to issues such as overuse, stress, and a decline in mental health.

The concept of a digital detox—a period of time when a person refrains from using digital devices such as smartphones, computers, and social media—has gained popularity as a way to combat these challenges. By stepping back from constant connectivity, individuals can reset their minds, improve their focus, and reduce anxiety related to the demands of the digital world.

In this chapter, we will explore the growing need for digital detoxes, their impact on mental health, and how to implement them effectively. We'll delve into the psychological effects of technology overuse, identify signs that a digital detox may be necessary, and offer practical strategies to reduce digital dependency. By the end of this chapter, readers will have a clear understanding of how to manage technology use for better mental health and overall well-being.

## Section 1: The Effects of Technology Overuse on Mental Health

While technology has revolutionized many aspects of daily life, its pervasive presence can lead to significant mental health challenges, particularly when used excessively. Here, we explore some of the primary ways technology impacts mental well-being.

### 1.1 The Anxiety of Constant Connectivity

Many people feel pressured to be constantly connected, whether it's through social media, email, or messaging apps. This constant need to be available and responsive can lead to heightened anxiety and stress.

- **Fear of Missing Out (FOMO):** Social media platforms exacerbate this anxiety by promoting a constant stream of updates, which can cause individuals to feel like they're missing out on events, experiences, or opportunities that others are enjoying. The desire to stay updated and engaged often leads to compulsive checking of apps and notifications.
- **Work-related stress:** With the rise of remote work and the expectation of being reachable at all times, many employees feel obligated to respond to work emails or messages outside of traditional work hours. This blurring of boundaries between work and personal time can result in chronic stress and burnout.

## 1.2 Impact on Sleep

Technology use, especially before bedtime, can disrupt sleep patterns. The blue light emitted by screens interferes with the production of melatonin, a hormone that regulates sleep. Additionally, engaging with stimulating content, such as social media or work emails, can make it harder to wind down and fall asleep.

- **Sleep deprivation:** Research shows that individuals who spend more time on screens–particularly before bed–are more likely to suffer from sleep disturbances, including insomnia. Poor sleep, in turn, affects mental health, leading to irritability, difficulty concentrating, and a heightened risk of anxiety and depression.

## 1.3 Digital Overload and Decision Fatigue

The sheer volume of information available online can lead to what is known as digital overload. With endless choices at our fingertips–whether it's selecting a movie, reading the news, or browsing social media feeds–many individuals experience decision fatigue, a state in which the brain becomes overwhelmed by the constant need to make decisions, both big and small.

- **Cognitive overload:** Constantly processing large amounts of information can lead to mental exhaustion. People may find it harder to focus, make decisions, or engage in deep thinking after prolonged exposure to digital content.

### 1.4 Social Comparison and Low Self-Esteem

Social media platforms often encourage users to compare their lives to the curated and idealized images they see online. This can lead to feelings of inadequacy, envy, and low self-esteem, particularly for individuals who are vulnerable to external validation.

- **The comparison trap:** Many people struggle with comparing their achievements, appearances, or relationships to those depicted on social media. Over time, these comparisons can erode self-worth and contribute to the development of anxiety and depression.

### 1.5 Decreased Attention Span and Productivity

Constant exposure to notifications and multitasking between apps can weaken the brain's ability to focus for extended periods. Studies have shown that frequent interruptions from notifications or the habit of switching between tasks online can lead to reduced attention span and decreased productivity.

- **Multitasking myth:** While many believe that multitasking makes them more productive, research suggests that the brain performs better when focusing on one task at a time. Attempting to juggle multiple tasks simultaneously can reduce efficiency and increase cognitive stress.

## Section 2: Signs That a Digital Detox May Be Necessary

Before diving into strategies for a digital detox, it's important to recognize when a break from technology might be needed. Here are some common signs that digital overuse is negatively impacting mental health:

### 2.1 Feeling Overwhelmed or Anxious

If you frequently feel overwhelmed by the number of messages, notifications, or updates you receive, or if you feel anxious about keeping up with everything, it may be time for a digital detox. This constant connectivity can take a toll on your emotional well-being, leading to heightened stress levels.

### 2.2 Struggling to Focus or Be Present

Do you find it difficult to focus on conversations, tasks, or activities without reaching for your phone? Are you constantly distracted by your device, even during important moments? This lack of presence, both mentally and emotionally, can damage relationships and reduce overall life satisfaction.

### 2.3 Sleep Problems

If your sleep has been affected by late-night scrolling, excessive screen time, or work-related stress from constant digital communication, it may be time to step back from technology.

### 2.4 Declining Mental or Physical Health

If you've noticed a decline in your mental health, such as increased feelings of loneliness, irritability, anxiety, or depression, technology may be a contributing factor. Likewise, if you've become more sedentary due to prolonged screen time, this can affect your physical health, contributing to issues such as poor posture, weight gain, and chronic fatigue.

### 2.5 Increased Dependence on Technology

If you feel a compulsive need to check your phone, social media, or work emails—even when there's no pressing reason to do so—you may be developing a dependence on technology. This can interfere with daily life and reduce your ability to relax or enjoy non-digital activities.

## Section 3: The Benefits of a Digital Detox

Engaging in a digital detox can provide numerous benefits, both for mental health and overall well-being. Here's how stepping back from technology can improve your life:

### 3.1 Improved Mental Clarity and Focus

A break from technology allows the brain to reset, reducing the cognitive overload caused by constant multitasking and digital distractions. This can improve concentration, enhance decision-making, and allow for more creative thinking.

### 3.2 Better Sleep Quality

Disconnecting from screens, particularly in the evening, can significantly improve sleep quality. Without the interference of blue light and the stimulation of digital content, the brain can produce melatonin more effectively, leading to deeper, more restorative sleep.

### 3.3 Enhanced Relationships

By stepping away from devices, you can be more present and engaged in your personal relationships. A digital detox creates more opportunities for meaningful conversations, quality time, and connection with loved ones, without the interruptions of notifications or work-related distractions.

### 3.4 Reduced Anxiety and Stress

A break from constant connectivity can reduce the anxiety and stress associated with always being "on." Without the pressure to respond to messages or keep up with social media, individuals often feel more relaxed and at peace.

### 3.5 Increased Productivity

Without the distractions of digital devices, individuals often find that they are more productive. They can focus more deeply on tasks, work more efficiently, and complete projects with greater satisfaction.

### 3.6 Greater Appreciation for Offline Activities

A digital detox encourages individuals to rediscover offline hobbies and activities, such as reading, hiking, cooking, or spending time with loved ones. These activities provide a sense of fulfillment and joy that is often missing in the digital world.

## Section 4: How to Implement a Successful Digital Detox

Now that we understand the signs of digital overuse and the benefits of taking a break, let's explore practical steps for implementing a digital detox. It's important to approach a digital detox in a way that feels manageable and sustainable, rather than overwhelming.

### 4.1 Start Small: Set Clear Goals

The idea of completely disconnecting from technology can feel daunting, especially if you rely on it for work or communication. Instead of attempting a full detox immediately, start small by setting specific goals.

- **Limit screen time:** Begin by setting daily limits on non-essential screen time, such as social media or entertainment apps. You can use screen time tracking tools to help monitor your usage.
- **Designate tech-free hours:** Choose certain times of the day when you will refrain from using digital devices. For example, you could implement a "no-phone rule" during meals or before bedtime.

### 4.2 Create Tech-Free Zones

Designate specific areas of your home or workspace as tech-free zones, where no devices are allowed. This could include the dining room, bedroom, or a designated reading or relaxation space.

- **Bedroom boundaries:** Keeping digital devices out of the bedroom can greatly improve sleep quality and mental relaxation. Use an alarm clock instead of your phone to avoid the temptation of late-night scrolling.

### 4.3 Schedule Regular Breaks from Technology

Incorporating regular breaks from technology into your routine can make a big difference in your mental health. This can include daily, weekly, or even longer-term breaks, depending on your needs.

- **Daily breaks:** Implement short digital detoxes throughout your day, such as taking a walk without your phone or spending 30 minutes doing a non-digital activity.
- **Weekend detoxes:** Consider dedicating one day or weekend per month to a full digital detox, where you unplug from all devices and spend time doing offline activities.

### 4.4 Practice Mindfulness with Technology Use

Rather than using technology mindlessly, practice being more intentional with your digital habits. This means being aware of when and why you're using your devices, and recognizing when it's time to step away.

- **Mindful social media use:** Before opening a social media app, ask yourself why you're doing so. Are you bored, anxious, or seeking validation? Being mindful of your motives can help reduce compulsive use.
- **Single-tasking:** Focus on completing one task at a time, rather than switching between multiple apps

or tabs. This can improve your focus and productivity while reducing stress.

## Conclusion: Achieving Balance in a Digital World

A digital detox is not about rejecting technology altogether, but about finding a healthier, more balanced relationship with it. In a world where we are constantly bombarded with digital information, it's crucial to take intentional breaks to protect our mental health, enhance our focus, and reconnect with the people and activities that bring us joy.

By recognizing the signs of digital overload, understanding the benefits of stepping away, and implementing practical strategies for reducing screen time, we can create a more fulfilling and less stressful relationship with technology. A successful digital detox can lead to improved mental clarity, better sleep, deeper relationships, and a greater sense of control over your time and well-being.

# CHAPTER 11

# THE ROLE OF EXERCISE, NUTRITION, AND SLEEP IN WORK-LIFE BALANCE

Achieving work-life balance is a multifaceted challenge that involves more than just managing time between professional and personal responsibilities. It also requires taking care of your physical and mental health, as these aspects significantly affect your ability to perform well at work, maintain relationships, and enjoy a fulfilling personal life. Among the most critical factors influencing overall well-being are exercise, nutrition, and sleep—the three pillars that sustain physical health, mental clarity, and emotional resilience.

These pillars work together to form the foundation of a healthy, balanced life. When onc aspect is neglected, the others often suffer, leading to issues such as fatigue, stress, and burnout. In this chapter, we'll explore the interconnected roles of exercise, nutrition, and sleep in maintaining work-life balance and offer practical strategies to optimize each for a healthier, more productive, and balanced lifestyle.

## Section 1: The Importance of Exercise in Work-Life Balance

Exercise is essential not only for physical health but also for mental and emotional well-being. Regular physical activity can help manage stress, improve cognitive function, boost energy levels, and even enhance mood—factors that directly contribute to better work-life balance.

### 1.1 Physical Benefits of Regular Exercise

The physical benefits of exercise are well-documented. Engaging in regular physical activity helps maintain a healthy body weight, strengthens muscles and bones, improves cardiovascular health, and reduces the risk of chronic diseases such as diabetes, heart disease, and obesity. But how does this relate to work-life balance?

- **Increased energy levels:** Exercise stimulates the production of endorphins, which increase energy and reduce feelings of fatigue. Regular activity can improve stamina, helping you get through your workday with more vitality and still have energy left for personal activities in the evening.
- **Improved physical resilience:** A healthy body is more resilient to the physical effects of stress. Regular exercise strengthens the immune system, reduces inflammation, and lowers the body's cortisol levels, helping you recover more quickly from stressors in both your work and personal life.

### 1.2 Mental Health Benefits of Exercise

Exercise is one of the most effective ways to improve mental health. It can alleviate symptoms of anxiety, depression, and stress, all of which can negatively impact work-life balance if left unchecked.

- **Stress relief:** Physical activity reduces levels of cortisol, the body's stress hormone, and promotes the release of endorphins, chemicals that naturally improve mood and reduce pain. Regular exercise acts as a natural form of stress management, helping you stay calm and focused, even during demanding work periods.

- **Enhanced cognitive function:** Exercise has been shown to improve memory, learning, and concentration. This can lead to better performance at work, allowing you to complete tasks more efficiently, and freeing up more time for personal pursuits.
- **Mood regulation:** Regular exercise is linked to a reduction in symptoms of depression and anxiety. It can improve self-esteem, boost overall happiness, and create a positive feedback loop in which a healthier body leads to a healthier mind.

### 1.3 Incorporating Exercise into a Busy Schedule

For many people, one of the biggest challenges to maintaining a regular exercise routine is time. However, even with a busy schedule, it's possible to incorporate physical activity into your day. Here are some strategies:

- **Short, high-intensity workouts:** If you don't have time for long gym sessions, opt for high-intensity interval training (HIIT) or other quick workouts that can be done in 20-30 minutes. These shorter workouts can be just as effective as longer, lower-intensity ones.
- **Active commuting:** If possible, consider walking or cycling to work, or parking further away to add more physical activity to your daily routine.

- **Desk exercises and stretching:** Even if you have a desk job, you can incorporate movement throughout the day. Stand up to stretch, take short walks during breaks, or perform simple desk exercises to stay active and avoid the negative effects of prolonged sitting.

## Section 2: Nutrition and Its Role in Work-Life Balance

Nutrition plays a crucial role in fueling your body and mind. The food you consume directly affects your energy levels, cognitive function, mood, and overall health. When you nourish your body with the right nutrients, you are better equipped to handle the stresses of both work and personal life.

### 2.1 The Connection between Nutrition and Energy Levels

One of the most immediate ways that nutrition affects work-life balance is through its impact on energy levels. A balanced diet provides the fuel your body needs to function optimally, while poor dietary choices can lead to energy crashes, fatigue, and difficulty concentrating.

- **Balanced meals:** Eating a diet rich in complex carbohydrates, lean proteins, healthy fats, and plenty of fruits and vegetables can help maintain steady energy levels throughout the day. Avoiding processed foods, excessive sugar, and refined carbohydrates can prevent energy spikes and crashes that leave you feeling sluggish.

- **Hydration:** Staying hydrated is just as important as eating well. Even mild dehydration can cause fatigue, difficulty concentrating, and irritability. Drinking plenty of water throughout the day can help maintain physical and mental performance.

## 2.2 Nutrition and Mental Health

Just as food impacts physical energy, it also has a significant effect on mental health. Nutrient-dense foods can support brain function, stabilize mood, and reduce the risk of mental health disorders.

- **Brain-boosting nutrients:** Omega-3 fatty acids, found in foods such as fatty fish, walnuts, and flaxseeds, are known to support brain health and reduce symptoms of depression and anxiety. Likewise, vitamins and minerals such as vitamin D, magnesium, and B vitamins play crucial roles in regulating mood and cognitive function.
- **Avoiding the pitfalls of emotional eating:** When stressed, many people turn to comfort foods that are high in sugar, fat, or salt. While these foods may provide temporary relief, they can lead to energy crashes and exacerbate feelings of anxiety or depression. Mindful eating practices, such as paying attention to hunger and fullness cues, can help you make healthier choices even in times of stress.

## 2.3 Meal Planning for a Balanced Life

Incorporating healthy eating into a busy schedule can be challenging, but with a bit of planning, it's possible to maintain a nutritious diet even on the busiest days. Here are some strategies:

- **Meal prepping:** Dedicate a few hours each week to preparing meals in advance. Cooking in batches allows you to have healthy, balanced meals ready to go, reducing the temptation to grab fast food or skip meals when you're pressed for time.
- **Healthy snacking:** Keep healthy snacks, such as fruits, nuts, yogurt, or vegetables with hummus, on hand to maintain energy levels between meals. Avoid reaching for sugary or processed snacks that can lead to energy crashes later in the day.
- **Eating mindfully:** Taking the time to eat meals without distractions (such as working through lunch or scrolling on your phone) can improve digestion and help you enjoy your food more, making it easier to maintain healthy eating habits.

## Section 3: The Critical Role of Sleep in Work-Life Balance

Of the three pillars—exercise, nutrition, and sleep—sleep is often the most neglected, yet it plays a critical role in maintaining both physical and mental health. Without adequate sleep, even the best exercise and nutrition habits may not be enough to keep you functioning optimally. Sleep affects everything from energy levels and cognitive performance to mood and emotional resilience.

## 3.1 The Link between Sleep and Cognitive Performance

Sleep is essential for cognitive function, including memory, learning, decision-making, and problem-solving. During sleep, the brain consolidates new information and clears away toxins that accumulate during the day, allowing you to wake up refreshed and ready to take on new challenges.

- **Impaired performance:** Chronic sleep deprivation can impair attention, concentration, and creativity, making it harder to perform well at work. Lack of sleep also increases the likelihood of making mistakes and can reduce productivity.

## 3.2 Sleep and Emotional Regulation

Sleep also plays a crucial role in regulating emotions. Without sufficient rest, the brain's ability to manage stress and regulate mood is compromised.

- **Increased stress and irritability:** Sleep-deprived individuals are more likely to experience mood swings, irritability, and heightened stress levels. This can strain relationships and make it difficult to maintain work-life balance.
- **Risk of burnout:** Over time, a lack of sleep can contribute to burnout—a state of chronic physical and emotional exhaustion caused by prolonged stress.

### 3.3 Sleep Hygiene: How to Improve Sleep Quality

Good sleep hygiene involves creating habits and an environment that promote restful, restorative sleep. Here are some strategies for improving sleep quality:

- **Consistent sleep schedule:** Going to bed and waking up at the same time every day (even on weekends) helps regulate your body's internal clock and makes it easier to fall asleep and wake up feeling refreshed.
- **Create a bedtime routine:** Engage in relaxing activities before bed, such as reading, meditation, or gentle stretching, to signal to your brain that it's time to wind down.
- **Limit screen time before bed:** The blue light emitted by phones, computers, and TVs interferes with the production of melatonin, a hormone that regulates sleep. Avoid screens for at least an hour before bedtime.
- **Create a sleep-friendly environment:** Ensure that your bedroom is conducive to sleep by keeping it cool, dark, and quiet. Invest in a comfortable mattress and pillows, and consider using blackout curtains or a white noise machine if necessary.

### 3.4 Prioritizing Sleep despite a Busy Schedule

In a world that often prioritizes productivity over rest, many people sacrifice sleep to get more done. However, this is a counterproductive strategy, as poor sleep ultimately reduces efficiency and effectiveness. Here are some tips for making sleep a priority:

- **Set boundaries:** Establish firm boundaries between work and rest time. Avoid working late into the night, and set a cutoff time for work-related tasks so that you have enough time to unwind before bed.
- **Take short naps:** If you're struggling with sleep during particularly busy times, short naps (10-20 minutes) can help boost alertness and improve performance without interfering with your night time sleep.

## Conclusion: A Holistic Approach to Work-Life Balance

Achieving work-life balance requires more than just time management–it demands a holistic approach that encompasses physical, mental, and emotional well-being. Exercise, nutrition, and sleep are the three pillars that sustain this balance. By prioritizing these aspects of your health, you'll not only improve your work performance but also enhance your personal life, creating a sense of balance that fosters long-term well-being.

Making small but consistent improvements in your exercise routine, dietary habits, and sleep hygiene can lead to significant changes in your overall quality of life. By investing in these foundational elements of health, you'll be better equipped to handle the stresses of work, enjoy meaningful personal relationships, and pursue your passions outside of work.

# CHAPTER 12

# NAVIGATING MAJOR LIFE TRANSITIONS WHILE MAINTAINING BALANCE

Life is full of transitions, both expected and unexpected. Whether it's starting a new job, moving to a new city, getting married, having children, or dealing with loss or illness, major life transitions often shake the foundations of our daily routines and challenge our ability to maintain a sense of balance. These periods of change can feel overwhelming as they typically bring new responsibilities, stress, and uncertainty. Balancing work, personal life, and mental health during these transitions can feel daunting, but with the right strategies and mindset, it is possible to navigate these changes while maintaining equilibrium.

In this chapter, we will explore various major life transitions, how they can impact your work-life balance, and effective strategies to help you navigate these periods with resilience and clarity. By understanding the nature of change and developing practical tools for coping with transitions, you can better manage the challenges they present while maintaining your well-being.

## Section 1: Understanding Life Transitions and Their Impact

Major life transitions often disrupt the normal flow of life, requiring adaptation, flexibility, and resilience. They can bring about feelings of excitement, stress, uncertainty, and sometimes fear. These transitions can be both positive and negative, but even positive changes such as a job promotion or the birth of a child can present challenges to your work-life balance.

### 1.1 Types of Major Life Transitions

Some of the most common life transitions that can impact work-life balance include:

- **Career transitions:** Starting a new job, getting promoted, or changing industries can bring new responsibilities, increased workloads, and pressure to prove yourself, all of which can strain your balance between work and personal life.
- **Personal milestones:** Getting married, having children, or moving in with a partner are significant life events that bring joy and excitement but also require adjustments in time management, relationships, and personal priorities.
- **Relocation:** Moving to a new city or country for work or personal reasons disrupts your established routines and often involves emotional and logistical challenges such as finding new social connections, adjusting to a different environment, or dealing with homesickness.
- **Illness or loss:** Facing the illness or death of a loved one, or dealing with your own health challenges, can be emotionally draining and disrupt every aspect of life, from work to personal relationships.
- **Divorce or separation:** Ending a long-term relationship or marriage can be a profoundly

emotional and stressful experience. It often requires rethinking your routines, living arrangements, and support systems while still maintaining professional responsibilities.

## 1.2 The Emotional Impact of Transitions

Life transitions can evoke a wide range of emotions, from excitement and anticipation to anxiety, stress, and grief. Even positive changes can trigger feelings of loss or uncertainty, as they often involve leaving behind familiar roles, environments, or routines. Understanding the emotional impact of transitions is crucial to managing them effectively and preventing burnout or overwhelm.

- **Uncertainty:** Major transitions often bring uncertainty about the future, which can lead to feelings of anxiety and fear. Whether you're unsure about a new job or a new personal role, the unknown can feel destabilizing.
- **Identity shifts:** Transitions can involve changes in your sense of identity. For example, becoming a parent or leaving a long-term job can challenge your self-concept, requiring you to redefine who you are and how you relate to the world around you.
- **Stress and overwhelm:** Managing the logistics of a major life transition—whether it's coordinating a move, planning a wedding, or caring for a sick family member—can be stressful and overwhelming, especially when combined with professional responsibilities.

### 1.3 The Impact on Work-Life Balance

Major life transitions often throw off the delicate balance between work and personal life. These transitions can demand significant time, energy, and attention, making it difficult to maintain your usual routines. Common challenges include:

- **Time management:** Life transitions often require you to spend more time on personal matters, leaving less time for work or self-care. Balancing new responsibilities can feel like a juggling act.
- **Emotional exhaustion:** The emotional toll of a major life transition can affect your energy and focus, making it harder to perform well at work and maintain healthy personal relationships.
- **Shifting priorities:** During major life transitions, your priorities may change. What once seemed important—such as advancing your career—may take a backseat to more immediate personal concerns, like caring for a family member or adjusting to a new role.

## Section 2: Strategies for Navigating Major Life Transitions

While life transitions are often challenging, they also present opportunities for growth and self-discovery. By approaching transitions with intentionality and flexibility, you can successfully navigate these periods while maintaining a sense of balance. Below are strategies for managing different types of life transitions.

## 2.1 Embrace Change as an Opportunity for Growth

Change can be difficult, but it's also a natural part of life. Learning to view transitions as opportunities for growth, rather than obstacles, can help you approach them with a more positive and resilient mindset.

- **Reframe your perspective:** Instead of focusing on what you're losing during a transition, try to focus on what you're gaining. For example, a new job may be stressful, but it also presents opportunities for personal and professional growth.
- **Develop a growth mindset:** Embracing a growth mindset–the belief that challenges are opportunities to learn and grow–can help you stay resilient during times of change. Rather than resisting the transition, see it as a chance to develop new skills, habits, and perspectives.

## 2.2 Establish New Routines and Boundaries

During life transitions, your usual routines may be disrupted, and it can be easy to lose your sense of structure. One of the most effective ways to regain balance is by establishing new routines that accommodate your changing circumstances.

- **Create a new daily schedule:** Map out a new daily routine that balances your work responsibilities with your personal needs. This might involve setting aside specific times for work, self-care, and family time. A structured routine can help reduce feelings of overwhelm and provide a sense of stability during uncertain times.

- **Set boundaries:** Boundaries become especially important during life transitions, as new responsibilities and challenges arise. Be clear with yourself and others about what you can realistically manage, and don't be afraid to say no to additional tasks or requests that would stretch you too thin.

## 2.3 Prioritize Self-Care and Mental Health

Taking care of your mental and physical well-being is crucial when navigating a major life transition. During times of change, self-care can often fall by the wayside, but maintaining healthy habits is essential for managing stress and maintaining balance.

- **Practice mindfulness:** Mindfulness practices, such as meditation or deep breathing, can help you stay grounded and reduce stress during periods of change. Mindfulness allows you to focus on the present moment, rather than worrying about the future.
- **Schedule self-care:** Treat self-care as a non-negotiable part of your routine. Whether it's exercising, spending time in nature, or engaging in a creative hobby, regular self-care practices can help you recharge and maintain emotional balance.
- **Seek support:** Don't be afraid to reach out to friends, family, or a therapist for support during a transition. Talking through your feelings with others can provide emotional relief and offer new perspectives on your situation.

## 2.4 Maintain Communication in Personal and Professional Relationships

Life transitions often affect not just you, but also those around you–your family, friends, and colleagues. Maintaining open lines of communication is key to navigating these changes while keeping your relationships strong.

- **Be honest about your needs:** Whether it's asking for help at home or discussing a temporary adjustment to your work schedule, be honest with those around you about your needs. Clear communication helps manage expectations and reduces misunderstandings.
- **Update your manager or colleagues:** If your life transition is impacting your work, it's important to keep your employer informed. Discuss any necessary changes to your work hours, deadlines, or responsibilities to ensure that you're able to meet both personal and professional obligations.
- **Check in with loved ones:** Life transitions can put a strain on personal relationships, especially if both partners are experiencing significant changes. Regularly check in with your partner, family, or close friends to maintain connection and support each other through the transition.

## 2.5 Flexibility and Adaptability in the Face of Change

Life transitions rarely go exactly as planned, so it's important to remain flexible and adaptable. Expect that there will be challenges and setbacks, and approach them with a problem-solving mindset rather than frustration.

- **Be prepared for the unexpected:** Life transitions often come with surprises—whether it's a delayed move, an unexpected work project, or unplanned expenses. Rather than getting stressed by the unexpected, approach it with flexibility and a focus on finding solutions.
- **Adjust your goals:** During a transition, your long-term goals or plans may need to shift. Be open to adjusting your expectations, both for yourself and others, and recognize that balance may look different during periods of significant change.

## Section 3: Specific Strategies for Common Life Transitions

While the general strategies outlined above can apply to most life transitions, certain transitions present unique challenges. Below, we'll explore some specific strategies for navigating common types of life transitions.

### 3.1 Navigating Career Transitions

Changing jobs or moving to a new role within your company can be exciting but also stressful. To maintain work-life balance during a career transition:

- **Allow time for adjustment:** Understand that it will take time to adjust to new responsibilities, colleagues, or a new work environment. Be patient with yourself as you learn the ropes.

- **Set realistic expectations:** Don't expect to master your new role immediately. Focus on making steady progress rather than trying to prove yourself all at once.
- **Seek mentorship:** If you're entering a new field or role, seek out mentors who can offer advice and guidance during your transition. Having a support system at work can make the transition smoother and less stressful.

### 3.2 Managing Parenthood and Family Transitions

Becoming a parent or experiencing changes in family dynamics requires careful attention to balancing work and home life.

- **Create a support network:** Lean on family, friends, or hired help to support you during the transition to parenthood. Don't feel like you have to do everything on your own.
- **Take advantage of parental leave:** If available, use parental leave to focus on your family during this transition. This time allows you to adjust to your new responsibilities without the added pressure of work.
- **Communicate with your partner:** Open communication with your partner about dividing household and parenting responsibilities is essential for maintaining balance.

### 3.3 Coping with Illness or Loss

Facing illness, whether your own or a loved one's, can be emotionally and physically draining. During this difficult transition:

- **Prioritize rest and recovery:** If you're dealing with illness, prioritize rest and recovery over work tasks. Listen to your body and take the necessary time off.

- **Delegate tasks:** If you're caring for a loved one, delegate tasks where possible, whether at work or home. Ask for help from colleagues, family, or professional caregivers to avoid burnout.

- **Seek grief counseling:** If you're coping with the loss of a loved one, consider seeking counseling to process your emotions and navigate the grieving process while managing work responsibilities.

## Conclusion: Embracing Life Transitions with Balance

Major life transitions are inevitable, but they don't have to derail your sense of balance. By approaching these transitions with intention, flexibility, and self-compassion, you can navigate even the most challenging changes while maintaining your mental health and work-life balance. Embrace these periods of transition as opportunities for growth, and remember that it's okay to seek support when needed. With the right strategies in place, you can emerge from life transitions stronger, more resilient, and with a renewed sense of purpose.

# FINAL CHAPTER

# THE CONCLUSION: ACHIEVING SUSTAINABLE WORK-LIFE BALANCE

Achieving a sustainable work-life balance is one of the most challenging yet crucial aspects of modern life. It's not merely about dividing time evenly between professional and personal responsibilities but rather about aligning your actions with your values in a way that is fulfilling, manageable, and long-lasting. This intricate balance involves constantly shifting priorities, self-awareness, and setting realistic expectations in both areas of life.

Sustainable work-life balance goes beyond time management. It touches every part of life, from emotional and physical well-being to mental resilience, career ambitions, and personal relationships. Each person's journey toward balance is unique, making it important to tailor your approach according to your specific needs and circumstances. Over the long term, achieving balance means minimizing stress and burnout while enhancing productivity, health, and overall happiness.

In this conclusion, we will explore not just the idea of work-life balance but the detailed principles, strategies, and long-term effects of achieving this balance in a sustainable way. We'll delve deeper into the core areas where balance is often disrupted and how to maintain it over time, ensuring you can thrive in both personal and professional realms.

## Section 1: Understanding Sustainable Work-Life Balance

### 1.1 The Fluid Nature of Work-Life Balance

Many people picture work-life balance as a stable, unchanging state where work and personal life are perfectly synchronized. However, this concept is fluid and requires continuous adjustments depending on changing circumstances. Work-life balance is never static—it fluctuates depending on your workload, personal commitments, health, and even unexpected life events.

For instance, during certain periods, such as when working on an important project or preparing for a promotion, your professional life may dominate. On the other hand, there may be times when personal life takes precedence, such as when dealing with family responsibilities, illness, or major life events like getting married or having a child.

Understanding the fluidity of work-life balance helps prevent frustration or guilt when one aspect of life demands more attention. The goal is not to achieve a perfect balance every day, but to create a long-term equilibrium where neither work nor life consistently overshadows the other. To achieve this, flexibility is key—being adaptable to these shifts and reassessing priorities regularly helps keep stress at bay while allowing for sustainable progress in both areas.

### 1.2 Prioritization as the Foundation of Balance

Prioritization is at the heart of sustainable work-life balance. Given that time and energy are finite resources, how you allocate them determines whether you feel in control or overwhelmed. Prioritization involves making intentional choices based on what matters most to you at any given time. Rather than trying to do everything, focus on the tasks and activities that align with your core values and long-term goals.

Effective prioritization starts with understanding your personal and professional values. Once you know what's most important—whether it's family, career advancement, self-care, or personal development—you can organize your time accordingly. For instance, if spending quality time with family is a top priority, make sure your work schedule allows for that, even if it means saying no to extra projects or overtime.

Additionally, tools like Eisenhower's Urgent-Important Matrix can help you categorize tasks into four quadrants: urgent and important, important but not urgent, urgent but not important, and neither urgent nor important. This approach ensures that you spend time on what truly matters rather than constantly reacting to the most immediate demands, which may not align with your overall priorities.

### 1.3 Balance vs. Integration

In recent years, the concept of work-life integration has emerged as an alternative to work-life balance. Instead of viewing work and life as two separate entities that need to be balanced, work-life integration acknowledges that these spheres often overlap. Especially in an era of remote work and flexible schedules, many people are finding that work and personal life naturally blend together.

Work-life integration means finding harmony between professional and personal responsibilities rather than trying to compartmentalize them. For example, you might take a midday break to attend to personal matters, such as picking up your child from school or running an errand, then return to work later in the evening when you're more focused.

This approach can be highly effective, particularly for individuals who have flexible jobs or work from home. However, work-life integration requires clear boundaries to ensure that work doesn't dominate personal life. Setting limits on work hours, carving out personal time, and ensuring that you're mentally and emotionally present for personal moments are essential to making this model sustainable.

## Section 2: Common Obstacles to Work-Life Balance

### 2.1 Overcommitment and Lack of Boundaries

One of the most common obstacles to achieving work-life balance is overcommitment, which often stems from an inability to set boundaries. People frequently take on more responsibilities than they can reasonably manage, whether it's accepting additional work assignments, volunteering for extra duties, or committing to too many social engagements. Overcommitment leads to exhaustion, burnout, and a persistent feeling of being overwhelmed.

A lack of boundaries between work and personal life compounds the problem. In today's always-on culture, it's easy for work to spill over into personal time. Whether it's checking emails during family dinners, taking work calls late at night, or bringing work stress home, the blurring of boundaries makes it difficult to disconnect and recharge.

Setting clear boundaries is a crucial strategy for overcoming overcommitment. This involves learning to say no to additional responsibilities that don't align with your priorities, scheduling time for personal activities, and creating a mental separation between work and home life. For instance, establish specific hours when you will not engage in work-related activities, and stick to them. Over time, these boundaries will help you protect your time and energy, allowing for more balance and fulfillment in both areas of life.

## 2.2 Technology and Constant Connectivity

While technology has transformed the way we work, it has also contributed to the erosion of work-life balance. Smartphones, email, messaging apps, and video conferencing tools enable constant communication, which can make it difficult to disconnect from work. Even when people leave the office, they are often still reachable by phone, email, or text, creating an expectation that they should be available at all times.

This constant connectivity leads to a state of "always-on" work mode, where employees feel pressured to respond to messages, attend meetings, or check emails outside of regular working hours. As a result, personal time is often interrupted by work obligations, leading to increased stress and a reduced ability to relax and recharge.

To combat the effects of constant connectivity, it's important to establish digital boundaries. This might involve turning off email notifications after work hours, setting specific times during the day to check messages, or using apps that limit screen time. Implementing regular "digital detoxes" where you disconnect from technology for an extended period can also help reset your relationship with work and create a clearer separation between your professional and personal life.

### 2.3 Lack of Support Systems

A lack of support–both in the workplace and in personal life–can be a significant barrier to achieving work-life balance. When individuals feel like they have to manage everything on their own, whether it's job responsibilities, household tasks, or caregiving, the burden can become overwhelming.

In the workplace, a lack of flexibility or understanding from managers can exacerbate work-life balance issues. If employees are not given the tools, resources, or flexibility they need to manage their workloads, they may struggle to meet both professional and personal obligations. Similarly, at home, if individuals don't have help with tasks such as childcare, housework, or emotional support from family and friends, it becomes difficult to create balance.

Building and maintaining support systems is key to overcoming this obstacle. At work, this might involve advocating for more flexible working arrangements, seeking mentorship, or collaborating with colleagues to share the workload. In personal life, it might mean asking for help from family members, hiring assistance for household tasks, or connecting with a support network of friends and community members.

## 2.4 Perfectionism and Unrealistic Expectations

Perfectionism is one of the biggest barriers to work-life balance. The desire to do everything perfectly can lead to overworking, overcommitting, and a constant feeling of inadequacy. Perfectionists often have unrealistic expectations of themselves, believing that they must excel in every aspect of life—whether it's at work, at home, or in personal relationships. This mindset creates enormous pressure, leading to burnout and a diminished ability to enjoy life.

Overcoming perfectionism requires a mindset shift. Instead of striving for perfection, aim for progress and self-compassion. Recognize that mistakes and imperfections are a natural part of life and that it's okay to let go of the need for constant achievement. Setting realistic goals and managing expectations—both of yourself and others—can help reduce the pressure to be perfect and make work-life balance more attainable.

## Section 3: Strategies for Achieving Sustainable Work-Life Balance

### 3.1 Time Management and Planning

Time management is a cornerstone of work-life balance. With only 24 hours in a day, how you manage your time determines whether you're able to balance work, personal responsibilities, and self-care. Effective time management involves more than just creating to-do lists; it requires strategic planning and the ability to prioritize what matters most.

- **Setting Clear Goals:** Clearly define your personal and professional goals. This helps you focus your time on activities that bring you closer to achieving those goals. Without clear objectives, it's easy to get lost in busy work that doesn't align with your long-term vision.
- **Time-Blocking:** Time-blocking is a highly effective method of time management. By allocating specific blocks of time to different tasks or activities, you can ensure that both work and personal responsibilities receive attention. For example, you might block off two hours in the morning for deep work, followed by a one-hour block for personal errands, and so on.
- **Utilizing Technology Wisely:** Use productivity apps and tools to help manage your time efficiently. Calendar apps, task management software, and project management tools can help you stay organized and on track. However, be mindful not to over-rely on technology—digital distractions can easily derail your efforts if not managed properly.

## 3.2 Setting Boundaries

Boundaries are essential for maintaining balance. Without clear boundaries, work can easily encroach on personal time, and vice versa. Setting boundaries helps protect your time and ensures that you can dedicate yourself fully to both your professional and personal life when needed.

- **Work Boundaries:** Establish firm work hours and stick to them. Communicate these boundaries clearly to colleagues and supervisors, and resist the temptation to check emails or engage in work activities during your off-hours. If necessary, turn off work notifications outside of work hours to avoid distractions.
- **Personal Boundaries:** Just as you set boundaries at work, it's important to set boundaries in your personal life as well. This might mean saying no to social invitations when you need downtime, or setting limits on how much personal information you share with coworkers to maintain a healthy separation between work and life.
- **Self-Care Boundaries:** Prioritize self-care and make it non-negotiable. This includes scheduling time for activities that recharge you, such as exercise, hobbies, or spending time with loved ones. Treat these activities as essential parts of your routine, not optional extras.

## 3.3 Self-Care and Well-Being

Sustainable work-life balance is impossible without prioritizing your own well-being. Self-care is not a luxury but a necessity for maintaining mental, emotional, and physical health. Without adequate self-care, it's easy to become overwhelmed and burn out, making it difficult to manage both work and personal responsibilities.

- **Physical Health:** Regular exercise, a healthy diet, and sufficient sleep are critical components of self-care. Physical health directly impacts your energy levels, focus, and overall well-being, making it easier to manage stress and maintain balance.
- **Mental Health:** Mindfulness practices, such as meditation, journaling, or deep breathing exercises, can help you manage stress and stay centered amidst the demands of work and personal life. Regularly check in with yourself and seek support from a therapist or counselor if needed.
- **Emotional Well-Being:** Strong emotional well-being is built through nurturing personal relationships, engaging in activities that bring joy, and practicing self-compassion. Make time for friends, family, and hobbies that enrich your life and provide emotional support.

## 3.4 Communicating Your Needs

Open and honest communication is key to achieving sustainable work-life balance. Whether at work or at home, it's important to clearly communicate your needs, boundaries, and expectations to others.

- **Workplace Communication:** If you need more flexibility or support at work, don't hesitate to have a conversation with your supervisor. Be proactive about discussing your workload, deadlines, and any challenges you may be facing. Many employers are willing to offer flexible work arrangements if they understand your needs.

- **Home Communication:** At home, communicate with your family and loved ones about your responsibilities and how they can support you. Sharing the load–whether it's household chores, childcare, or emotional support–can alleviate stress and help you maintain balance.

### 3.5 Embracing Flexibility and Adaptability

Flexibility and adaptability are essential for maintaining long-term work-life balance. Life is unpredictable, and your ability to adjust your schedule, priorities, and expectations in response to changing circumstances is key to staying balanced.

- **Letting Go of Perfectionism:** Perfectionism is the enemy of balance. Instead of striving for perfection in every area of life, embrace the concept of "good enough." Allow yourself to make mistakes, learn from them, and move on without dwelling on perfection.
- **Regularly Reassessing Balance:** Work-life balance is not a one-time achievement–it's an ongoing process that requires regular evaluation and adjustment. Take time to assess your balance periodically, identify areas where you may be struggling, and make necessary changes to ensure you stay aligned with your priorities.

## Section 4: The Long-Term Benefits of Work-Life Balance

### 4.1 Improved Mental and Emotional Well-Being

Maintaining work-life balance has significant long-term benefits for your mental and emotional well-being. When work and life are in balance, you experience less chronic stress and anxiety, leading to improved mental clarity, emotional stability, and overall happiness.

- **Reduced Risk of Burnout:** Work-life balance prevents burnout by ensuring that you're not constantly overworking or neglecting your personal needs. By giving yourself time to rest, recharge, and engage in activities you enjoy, you reduce the risk of becoming physically and emotionally exhausted.
- **Enhanced Emotional Resilience:** With a balanced life, you're better equipped to handle challenges and setbacks, both at work and in your personal life. Emotional resilience comes from having the time and space to process emotions, reflect on experiences, and seek support when needed.

### 4.2 Increased Productivity and Performance

Contrary to the belief that working longer hours leads to greater productivity, research shows that overwork can actually reduce efficiency and performance. When you're well-rested and balanced, you're more focused, creative, and productive.

- **Enhanced Focus and Creativity:** A balanced life allows you to bring your best self to work. When you're not constantly stressed or overwhelmed, you're more focused, attentive, and creative in your work. This leads to higher-quality output and greater satisfaction in your professional achievements.
- **Sustainable Career Growth:** By prioritizing balance, you set yourself up for long-term career success. Rather than burning out from overwork, you maintain the energy, motivation, and enthusiasm needed to continue growing in your career over time.

### 4.3 Stronger Personal Relationships

Work-life balance allows you to nurture your personal relationships, which in turn provides emotional support and fulfillment. Strong relationships are a key component of overall happiness and well-being.

- **Improved Communication and Connection:** When you have time to invest in personal relationships, you build stronger connections with loved ones. This leads to more meaningful interactions, better communication, and a deeper sense of emotional intimacy with those closest to you.
- **Greater Relationship Satisfaction:** Achieving work-life balance enhances your ability to be present in your relationships, which leads to greater satisfaction and harmony in both romantic and familial relationships.

## 4.4 Long-Term Career Satisfaction

Achieving sustainable work-life balance allows you to pursue your career goals without sacrificing your personal life. Over time, this leads to greater job satisfaction, as you're able to excel in your career while maintaining a fulfilling personal life.

- **Avoiding Career Burnout:** Balancing work with personal time helps you avoid career burnout, ensuring that you have the energy and passion to continue pursuing your professional goals without feeling overwhelmed.
- **Maintaining Motivation:** Long-term career satisfaction comes from finding a sustainable pace at which to work. By setting realistic expectations, prioritizing self-care, and making time for personal interests, you maintain the motivation to succeed in your career without sacrificing your well-being.

## Final Thoughts: Embracing Balance as a Lifelong Practice

Achieving sustainable work-life balance is not a one-time goal but a lifelong practice. It requires continuous effort, self-reflection, and adaptability. By prioritizing your well-being, setting boundaries, and embracing flexibility, you can create a balanced life that supports both your personal happiness and professional success.

Remember that balance is not about perfection–it's about finding a rhythm that works for you and allows you to thrive in all areas of life. As you navigate the complexities of work, relationships, and personal growth, keep in mind that balance is an evolving process. Be patient with yourself, and allow your definition of balance to change as your life and priorities change.

With the right strategies and mindset, sustainable work-life balance is not only achievable but can lead to a more fulfilling and meaningful life. Embrace the journey, and remember that balance is a practice worth cultivating every day.